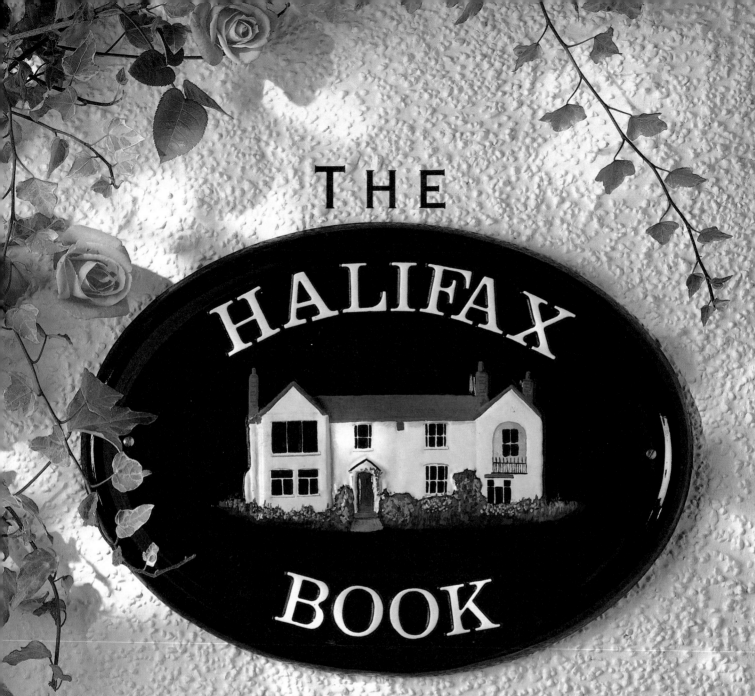

THE
HALIFAX
BOOK
OF HOME
IMPROVEMENTS

BILL EYKYN

First published in Great Britain in 1987
by Phoenix Publishing Assoc. Ltd.
Bushey, Herts.

Printed in Italy by Motta

Art Direction and Book Design
Ivor Claydon/Bob Hook
Sunset Design Co. Ltd

Typesetting by
Prestige Press (UK) Ltd

CONTENTS

AUTHOR'S ACKNOWLEDGEMENT

The author wishes to acknowledge the considerable help and encouragement given by his friend and colleague Ann Scutcher, Editorial Director of Home & Law Magazines. Her particular contribution to the kitchen, bathroom and other chapters concerning the rooms of a house is evidence of why *Exchange Contracts*, of which she is editor, is the leading home buyers' magazine in this country.

It is estimated that by the end of this century at least three quarters of all homes in the United Kingdom will be privately owned. Of course, home ownership brings with it the responsibility for maintenance and repairs.

The Halifax Building Society has a firm commitment to the provision of finance for home improvements and is keen to support any initiative which will encourage home owners to preserve, maintain and improve their properties. As such, the Society is pleased to be associated with this book which aims to provide accurate information on a multitude of home improvement matters and which should prove an invaluable source of reference for any home owner.

J D BIRRELL
OPERATIONS DIRECTOR

A HOME FOR IMPROVEMENT

The art of home improvement is to retain the essential character of the property while incorporating alterations or extensions to suit your way of life. Whatever you have in mind, your best starting point is with your building society.

The glorious thing about our architectural heritage is not so much the supreme collection of 'Great Houses', visited by millions of tourists each year, but our wealth of period property, lived in by millions of ordinary people earning their daily bread. It is a remarkable fact that a third of our national housing stock was built before the First World War and even half was built before the Second World War.

We still have pretty villages with Elizabethan cottages and Jacobean manor houses, towns with Queen Anne and early Georgian houses, cities full of eighteenth century architecture, whole streets of typical Victorian houses. There are thousands of Edwardian terraces and villas and millions of sturdy, between-the-wars properties – all with a great deal more character than many of the modern, soulless units claiming to be 'luxury development'.

The nation has had to learn the hard way that people don't like high-rise living in glass and concrete and, to a great extent, local authorities now try and refurbish rather than replace. In fact, there are 'listed' buildings which are not a century old, but how much property built today will be listed in a hundred years time?

While it is the character of older properties which is so endearing, often the internal layout and arrangement of the services are totally unsuited to the modern way of life. The challenge of an older house is to preserve its essential character while improving its amenities to suit the way you and your family wish to live. The art is to balance the old with the new, while the science is to achieve it in the most cost-effective manner. The opportunity is open to anyone inclined to take it, because the finance is usually available over a timescale which can suit

all kinds of personal circumstances. All that is necessary is the willingness to devote the time and the energy to make a success of it all.

RAISING THE MONEY

Whether you want to buy an old property and do it up, or you already own a property which is in need of improvement, the first thing you must do is to sort out the finances. Buying a house is obviously a greater step than developing a property you already own, but both demand an exercise in financial planning. In either case it is a matter of the property standing as collateral for the funds needed to develop it into just the type of home you want – and a more valuable asset as well.

For the whole exercise to be successful, you will find that everything hinges on *judgement* – both yours and other people's. You have to trust your own judgement of course, but this should extend to choosing the inevitably numerous people who will be involved – and upon whose specialist judgement you must rely. Whatever your natural demeanour, you will find it better to be slightly sceptical and safe rather than all smiles and sorry later!

Buying a house in good condition and in a state in which you are happy to live – save only a bit of redecoration – is a fairly straightforward matter. Its market value is likely to be determined by the going rate for the area, at a price upon which both parties should have little difficulty agreeing. However, buying a house in need of repairs and refurbishment, as well as further structural alterations to suit your requirements, is much more involved and not so readily agreed. You may, therefore, be involved in a few false starts before you find the property you want at a price you can afford.

The first thing to do is to reach an agreement, in principle, with whoever will be granting you the mortgage on which the whole transaction relies. For most of us this will be the manager of the local building society branch. If you are prudent you will already have a savings account with the society concerned, because in times when mortgage funds are scarce, those who have been saving with, for example, the Halifax, for a reasonable period of time will find that they are given preferential consideration.

The Halifax will normally be able to lend up to 80 per cent (sometimes even 100 per cent) of the purchase price or the Society's valuation of the property, whichever is the lower. In the case of an older property which needs attention and for which you have additional plans to improve, you will need to show the Society and its valuer that the additional money spent on the property will, indeed, increase its market value. Apart from anything else, the valuer will probably insist that certain defects be corrected as a condition of the mortgage offer. What is certain is that you are going to have to put up around 20 per cent as well as proving satisfactorily that you can repay the total mortgage you are seeking.

Therefore, it is essential that you have an early interview with the Society's manager to make an assessment of your situation. As a rough guide, the Halifax would normally consider a loan of up to three times your annual income, but this ratio varies according to the rate of interest currently being charged at the time of application. Overtime and bonuses can sometimes be taken into account if they are regular features of your income.

Where the property is to be purchased in joint names, both incomes can be taken into account on the basis of about three times the higher income plus the full amount of the lower income. Having established that a mortgage will be forthcoming, it's important now to consider which type of mortgage you should have.

DIFFERENT TYPES OF MORTGAGE

Basically there are two alternative types of home loan to choose from: a *repayment mortgage* and the life-assurance-linked mortgage usually called an *endowment mortgage*.

Repayment

With the repayment method, you make monthly payments made up of *level* instalments of capital and interest, over a fixed period of say 25 years. Illustrations of repayment costs usually show the tax relief based on an 'average' amount of interest, although of course there is much more interest in each of the earlier years' repayments, and much more capital in the repayments that are made in the later years. The actual tax relief will therefore be higher in the earlier years and lower in the later ones, but for comparison purposes the average system is not unfair.

With this type of mortgage you are recommended to take out an inexpensive mortgage protection or a similar life policy with an insurance company which would repay the loan should you – or either partner in a joint mortgage – die.

Endowment

Here the borrower pays only the interest to the lender, while he or she maintains an endowment policy which will pay off the capital of the loan at the end of the chosen period, or on his or her death before then. As with a repayment mortgage, full tax relief is obtained on the interest if the loan is £30,000 or less; if the loan is more than that amount then only up to £30,000.

The policy is assigned to the building society and the premium you pay is made direct to the insurance company, *after* deduction of tax. If there is a surplus at the end of the term, this belongs to you, the borrower, since the lender is entitled only to a return of what has been lent at the outset.

There are three principal variations of endowment policies:
1. *Endowment without profits*: Where an endowment assurance policy pays off precisely the amount borrowed, on the expiry of the loan, or on the borrower's earlier death. There are no bonuses.
2. *Endowment with profits*: Where the sum payable on death or on maturity will increase through bonuses every year so that after 15 years you might expect double the initial sum to be

paid on death or on maturity of the loan; after 25 years you should see about three and a half times the face value of the policy, on death or at expiry of the loan. This can provide substantial returns, which may be something of a luxury as the monthly premiums are higher.

3. *Low Cost Endowment*: Where a with-profits policy like that above is mixed with a term-assurance policy so the amount outstanding is covered throughout the period of the loan. At the end of the loan term there will be sufficient to repay the loan (unless bonuses have slumped) and there is usually a substantial bonus to the borrower. Meantime, the repayment cost has been even lower, assuming tax relief, than the average net monthly amount under the repayment period.

It is small wonder, therefore, that the low-cost endowment has become very widely used over the last few years. You should think seriously about such a plan if it is available to you, particularly since for fair comparison one should add the premium for a 'mortgage protection policy' to the cost of a repayment loan, increasing the net monthly cost by a pound or two.

It is very worthwhile considering additional forms of inexpensive protection which can be built into a policy, such as:

1. Joint life policies to repay the loan on the death of a husband or wife.

2. A health insurance element to ensure that premiums and interest payments will be maintained, even if the breadwinner is unable to work for a long time. With these you might feel protected against adversity and the Halifax, in common with most building societies, will help you obtain quotations.

Where part of the mortgage is intended to pay for the building works you are planning for the property in question, it will be essential for you to show that you know what is involved and have costed through the project carefully. This will mean preparing plans and estimates prior to the purchase of the property. Clearly, the estimates for the work, plus the purchase price being asked, must not amount to more than the savings you have and the mortgage you can afford. You will be fortunate indeed if it all works out on the first house you see!

Building societies are required by the Building Societies Act to obtain a written valuation in respect of any property offered as security for a mortgage. The Halifax offers mortgage applicants who are buying a home a choice of three different types of valuation and inspection reports:

Scheme 1 Report and Valuation for Mortgage Assessment which is a basic report primarily for the society's benefit but a copy of which will be sent to you for information.

Scheme 2 Report and Valuation for Home-Buyers which provides additional information on the state of repair and condition of the property. The report will be sent to you with a copy to the Halifax.

Scheme 3 Structural Survey Report which involves a more detailed examination of the property based on your instructions to the valuer.

It is most probable that the sort of property which needs remedial work and structural alterations will require a full structural survey. Obviously, to produce a comprehensive report on the condition of the property, describing in detail any structural or other defects, costs considerably more than a simple valuation or a general report. However, the professional findings of a full structural survey are indispensable to making the right decision on any property to which you intend making major alterations or improvements.

FULL STRUCTURAL SURVEY

When you are sure you want to buy the house, subject to a full structural survey, make certain you get the agreement of the vendor for the surveyor to have full and proper access to the property. There is nothing more infuriating than getting a surveyor's report which has limitations in every other paragraph because he was not able to 'take up a floorboard' or 'get into the roof space' or other such reasons. It may not, indeed, be practical to lift floorboards covered with parquet or on which vinyl has been stuck down, but most rooms will have carpets and there is no reason why they cannot be lifted. The surveyor will always make any restrictions to his access known in his report – but it still costs money and it's not helpful!

When you instruct your surveyor ask him to outline the scope of the survey, and let him know exactly what structural alterations you have in mind. He may, in any case, be able to give you preliminary advice on the work and a ball-park figure on the likely cost.

In his report the surveyor will note defects and recommend further opening up if he thinks it necessary. He will analyse such faults as he finds and recommend what action should be taken, as well as assessing possible future problems. His inspection will cover the structure and finishes of the building, outbuildings, garden fences and walls and nearby trees which might cause damage to buildings. He will usually include water services and drainage and report on the condition of the central heating and hot water system.

You should agree the basis of the fee at an early stage and find out if it covers travel, any builder's charges (perhaps for providing a long ladder for access to the roof or for carrying out a test to underground drains) and any specialist's charges (for example for inspecting foundations) and VAT. There is no set scale of fees so it is important to know what you are in for – before you commit yourself.

The good news is that a comprehensive structural survey may help to reduce the purchase price of the property, so that you can still afford to go ahead. The report may, however, reveal the bad news that it will all cost too much to do what you want with the property and so you will have to withdraw.

Even if you can forecast the cost of essential remedial work, what may not be so easy is to establish the *value* the improvements will add to the property after the work has been done. This really is one of those important matters of judgement – professional judgement in the shape of a written valuation by a qualified valuer appointed by the society.

HOME IMPROVEMENT LOAN

Given your house as a secure asset for three or four years, the difference between your outstanding mortgage and the market value might very well realise sufficient money to carry out some worthwhile improvements. For a relatively small additional premium tacked on to your existing mortgage repayments you could make your house more efficient and comfortable, while at the same time further increasing its value.

Furthermore, if your existing mortgage is below the current maximum (£30,000) allowable for tax relief, the Halifax Home Improvement Loan – added to the existing mortgage – will qualify for tax relief, provided only that the money is not used for repairs or replacements. When you come to sell your house at its enhanced value and your capital outlay is returned, the profit will not attract capital gains tax, so the whole exercise can clearly be a very worthwhile investment.

The way you approach your building society for a home improvement loan is important. In the 'Halifax House of Home Improvement' video (which is available on free loan to all Halifax account holders) the opening 'chapter' shows the sort of homework which is necessary to present a good case to a branch manager for a home improvement loan.

In that example a young married couple had bought a house for £31,000 with a Halifax mortgage three years previously and wanted to borrow £5,500 to improve their property to the same standard as a similar house 'just down the road' which had fetched £39,000 only a month before their interview.

The husband explained that his salary had increased because of a job promotion, while his wife was working again as a secretary now that the children were at school. The couple proved with their payslips that they could afford the increased repayments. With plans drawn up by a building surveyor and two estimates for the work, including an allowance for the fittings and a further contingency sum on top, the manager was soon convinced that the project was a sensible one – subject to a revaluation of the property by the Society.

The manager established other details concerning planning permission, building regulation control and the possibilities of a grant, as well as the necessary increase in the replacement value of the property for insurance purposes. By the end, the couple were completing their application form in the certain knowledge that the Society was only too pleased to help them finance their project.

LOCAL AUTHORITY GRANTS

It is always worth investigating whether or not you can get a local authority grant, but do not raise your hopes too high, as each authority has a different policy according to its political masters.

The amount you might get will depend on how much work you intend to do and where the property is, as well as the sort of work which is needed. The cost of any qualifying work is called the eligible expense and there are limits on the amount on which a grant can be paid.

All the figures quoted are not maximum grants, because what you will receive is a *percentage* of the eligible expense – anything extra you want to spend will not qualify. The council will decide what *rate of grant* to give you up to the maximum applying to your case

Homes that are in an unfit state, lacking standard amenities or in need of substantial and structural repair will receive a 75 per cent rate. So will houses in defined 'housing action areas' or those requiring improvement for a disabled person. Homes in general improvement areas can get 65 per cent and for all other cases 50 per cent.

While there are five different sorts of grants available, there is only one which you can bank on getting and even that has a title which seems designed to confuse – an *intermediate* grant.

INTERMEDIATE GRANTS

These grants are for putting in missing standard amenities (such as bath, basin

and wc where there was none installed before) into properties which were built before 1961. The grant is mandatory, so your local council cannot refuse you provided the property qualifies.

	Greater London	Else-where
Fixed bath or shower	£450	£340
Wash basin	£175	£130
Sink	£450	£340
Hot and cold water to:		
Fixed bath or shower	£570	£430
Wash basin	£300	£230
Sink	£380	£290
WC	£680	£515
Total	£3005	£2275

You can also get a grant towards the necessary repairs carried out at the same time as the installation work and you are not obliged to do all the work at one time. The council have the right to insist that, once the work is completed, the house or flat should be 'fit for human habitation' and you can claim the full repairs element of intermediate grant (eligible expense limit of £4,200 in Greater London and £3,000 elsewhere), in which case the council will normally require you to put the whole house or flat into reasonable repair. Alternatively you can claim a smaller amount for minor repairs against an expense limit of £420 per standard amenity in Greater London (subject to a maximum of £1,680) and £300 per standard amenity elsewhere (subject to a maximum of £1,200), in which case the house or flat will not have to meet any prescribed standard of repair.

REPAIR GRANTS

Repair grants are available only for houses or flats built before 1919 and are normally discretionary, so it is for your council to decide whether or not to give you a grant and if so at what rate. The works must be substantial and they must be structural (for example, major works to the roof, walls, floors or foundations). Routine work (like rewiring) or the replacement of worn fixtures (such as baths) will not qualify for a repairs grant.

The rateable value of the property must be under £400 in Greater London and under £225 elsewhere. The eligible expense limits are £6,600 in Greater London and £4,800 elsewhere – with higher limits applying to buildings which are listed as being of special architectural or historical interest.

IMPROVEMENT GRANTS

Improvement grants are discretionary, so again your local council may or may not give you one. Unless the property is in a housing action area or the grant is to improve a home for a disabled person, its rateable value must be less than £400 in Greater London or £225 elsewhere.

If you are fortunate enough to have an application approved, the amount you will get will be between 50 and 75 per cent of the eligible expense limits (£13,800 for priority cases and £9,000 for non-priority cases in Greater London and £10,200 and £6,600 respectively elsewhere) although in cases of hardship it is possible to get up to 90 per cent.

Houses or flats improved with the help of improvement grants will usually be expected to reach the standard set out below. But your council may agree to reduce the standard if they think it would be unreasonably expensive for the house or flat to meet all the requirements, or if they are satisfied that you could not pay for the work without a grant.

A house or flat will reach the standard referred to above, if after improvement, it will:
- Be likely to have a useful life of at least 30 years.
- Be in reasonable repair.
- Have all the standard amenities and meet the following requirements:
  1. Be substantially free from damp.
  2. Have adequate natural light and ventilation in each habitable room.
  3. Have adequate and safe provision throughout for artificial lighting and have sufficient electric socket outlets for the safe and proper functioning of domestic appliances.
  4. Be provided with adequate drainage facilities.
  5. Be in a stable structural condition.
  6. Have satisfactory internal arrangement.
  7. Have satisfactory facilities for preparing and cooking food.
  8. Be provided with adequate facilities for heating.
  9. Have proper provision for the storage of fuel (where necessary) and for the storage of refuse.
  10. Have adequate thermal insulation in the roof space.

SPECIAL GRANTS

These grants are for basic improvements and the provision of means of escape from fire in houses in multiple occupation. Within the context of this book it is not worth going into any detail about Special Grants, save only to say that they are normally discretionary and it is up to your council whether or not you can have one.

LOFT INSULATION GRANT

Providing the property was built before 1975 you can get a grant towards the cost of installing insulation in lofts of *any* dwelling where there is none already or where the existing amount is less than 30mm in depth. This means that if the loft is already insulated with the originally recommended thickness of 25mm (1 inch) or less, you may get a grant to put on a further layer of 100mm (4 inches). It also covers the insulation of water tanks and pipes in lofts and of uninsulated hot water cylinders wherever they are located.

Whilst only a small grant – £69 or 66 per cent of the total cost of the material and work, whichever is the smaller – it is certainly worth contacting your local council and getting an application form. For elderly or severely disabled applicants on low incomes the grant is increased to 90 per cent with a maximum of £95.

THE WORTH AND VALUE OF THE PROJECT

All property has two basic values: the market value and the rebuilding cost. The difference is important when considering the worth of the home improvements you have in mind and it is essential to establish both of them as part of your overall assessment.

MARKET VALUE

The market value of a property is simply what it will fetch on the open market. The price is determined by the location within an area, how desirable it is in itself, its relative value to similar properties and the current state of the property market at that particular time. In London, for example, a house in fashionable Knightsbridge may be three or four times as expensive as an exactly similar property a couple of miles away in Hammersmith; whereas a bigger, better property a hundred miles from the heart of the capital may fetch a fraction of the price.

By the same token, developing a property in London as opposed to a house in the north of England – with only a marginal difference in the building cost – may show a difference of tens of thousands of pounds in the relative market values.

REBUILDING COST

The rebuilding cost is usually less than the market value, because even if a house had to be totally rebuilt (because of a major fire, for example) the land is a permanent feature. Even so, rebuilding costs can vary considerably from property to property and from area to area. According to the Royal Institution of Chartered Surveyors, the biggest difference in cost per square foot – according to the type of house and location – indicates a maximum of £55 and a minimum of £30 per square foot. Therefore, although rebuilding costs may be as much as double when comparing one type of house or location with another, the variation is nowhere near the sort of differences in market values that are experienced around the country.

Consequently, it is important when you are buying a house to do up, or if you plan to improve or enlarge your present home, to investigate closely the proposed cost of your project and relate this to the market value of the property. The last thing you want to do is to overdevelop the property and find that you cannot recover your investment when the time comes to sell the house.

It is, therefore, well worthwhile visiting a number of local estate agents and seeing for yourself what properties like yours are currently fetching.

ESTATE AGENTS

Since anyone with a little money, no previous experience, no qualifications or any specific expertise can set themselves up as an estate agent, it is worth knowing how to sort out the trustworthy ones from the rest. It is particularly important when you are buying a house and will have to hand over a deposit. (It's amazing, when firms go into liquidation, how money on deposit for *anything* seems to be used for the benefit of the secured creditors rather than anyone else).

Many of the large, well-known firms of estate agents have the words

Protecting your investment: Good loft insulation is among the priorities when it comes to keeping your home comfortable and in good condition. Local authorities provide grants towards the cost of this important improvement project.

'chartered surveyors' after their name. This means that all the partners are individual members of the Royal Institution of Chartered Surveyors (RICS) and have only become so by way of examination and qualification.

The other long-standing professional body within estate agency is the Incorporated Society of Valuers & Auctioneers (ISVA) and you will see the designatory letters after partners' names on the letterheads of firms large and small.

A third and comparatively new organisation is the National Association of Estate Agents (NAEA) which was established in 1962. Membership of the Association is open to persons practising as estate agents, either by themselves or with others, as principals or employees of firms. Applicants for a corporate grade (with designatory letters after their name) are only considered after at least three years experience. By and large, members of the RICS and ISVA rely on their professional qualifications, whereas the bulk of NAEA members are drawn from outside the professional bodies.

DEPOSIT SAFETY

From your point of view, as a purchaser, all three organisations run bonding schemes to ensure adequate security for deposits left with an estate agent. The Estate Agents Act 1979 gives the Secretary of State the right to introduce compulsory bonding for all estate agents. However, maybe because of the high standards already set by the professions and the minimum cases of consequential loss, he has so far declined to take this step. Nevertheless, bonding is important and you should be aware of the security of your deposit in a client account with an estate agent. So do check – before you part with your money.

In the case of membership of the RICS, it is worth noting that the Institution has seven separate divisions, so that the appearance of the letters RICS after an individual's name does not actually tell you in which aspect of 'the land' the person specialises. The greatest number (42 per cent) are in what is called the General Practice Division where the surveyors 'are skilled in the valuation and management of all types of residential and commercial property for occupation or investment, also acting as agents on behalf of clients in its sale, purchase or leasing; specializations extend their services to the contents of buildings including furniture, works of art, plant and machinery'. It is members of this division who are in estate agency.

In chapter 3 the specific relevance of the Chartered Building Surveyor who 'advises owners on economic, legal, technical, structural and design aspects of buildings, on their potential and cost-effective maintenance when required' is considered carefully vis-a-vis the Chartered Architect and others whom you might consider when seeking a professional advisor for your home-improvement project.

It is as well to remember that estate agents do not normally make money *buying* houses for people, but rather in *selling* them. Since they are usually on commission it is in their interest to sell the property for as high a price as possible and if there are several people interested in buying the house they will be quick to point out the fact in the hope of getting you moving. However, if you are wanting to buy an older house that has undoubted defects it is important to tread carefully and not be rushed into something you might regret later.

It is important to visit the property on several occasions and at several different times of the day, so that you can appreciate all aspects of the house and area. Was the one aeroplane that went over just an occasional one or was it a particularly light day for traffic? Was the prevailing wind blowing when you were there or did the calm prevent the smell of the chicken farm reaching you? Did you visit it on a Sunday when there weren't many trains running on the nearby line? Were the next-door neighbour's noisy children at school or at home when you were shown over the house? Et cetera!

Remember, it is very easy when you have seen numerous properties over the last month or more to get all excited when you say to yourself or your spouse 'this is it – it's exactly what we've been looking for'. Say it in private – because a display of enthusiasm in front of the vendor or his agent will not help your negotiations over the price. With an older property on which much work must be done, you will need all the pennies you can raise.

INSURANCE AND SECURITY

Insurance and security are subject areas which you will need to include within your financial planning exercise. From the moment you purchase the property you must have adequate cover and protection. While the terms of your mortgage will insist on the buildings being insured, you also need to take into account the contents – and that means including security measures to stop a claim arising in the first place.

In the case of a mortgage with the Halifax the Society normally arranges your property insurance. The amount of cover will initially be the amount recommended by the Society's valuer as his estimate of the full replacement cost. However, to maintain protection of your home against inflation the figure is index-linked.

This means that the amount of cover changes each month with the house rebuilding cost index, but the premiums only change at renewal date. These are

How much would it cost to re-build your home? SEPTEMBER 1986 COSTINGS – £ PER SQUARE FOOT (EXTERNAL)									
DETACHED HOUSE		**PRE 1920**			**1920–1945**			**1946–DATE**		
		LARGE	MEDIUM	SMALL	LARGE	MEDIUM	SMALL	LARGE	MEDIUM	SMALL
	Region 1	50.50	55.00	53.50	48.50	50.50	51.00	41.50	44.00	44.00
	2	44.50	48.00	47.00	42.50	44.50	44.50	36.00	38.50	38.50
	3	42.00	45.50	44.50	40.50	42.00	42.50	34.50	36.50	36.50
	4	40.00	43.50	42.50	38.50	40.00	40.00	32.50	34.50	35.00
	Typical Area ft²	3450	1700	1300	2550	1350	1050	2550	1350	1050
SEMI-DETACHED										
	Region 1	49.50	50.50	50.50	52.50	50.50	50.50	37.50	40.00	42.50
	2	43.50	44.50	44.00	46.00	44.50	44.50	33.00	35.00	37.50
	3	41.50	42.00	42.00	43.50	42.00	42.00	31.50	33.50	35.50
	4	39.00	40.00	40.00	41.50	40.00	40.00	30.00	31.50	33.50
	Typical Area ft²	2300	1650	1200	1350	1150	900	1650	1350	1050
DETACHED BUNGALOW	Region 1				52.50	48.50	49.50	45.00	45.50	47.00
	2				46.00	42.50	43.50	39.50	39.50	41.50
	3				43.50	40.50	41.50	37.50	37.50	39.00
	4	The chart does not cover pre-1920 bungalows, as few such properties were built.			41.50	38.50	39.50	35.50	35.50	37.00
	Typical Area ft²				1650	1400	1000	2500	1350	1000
SEMI-DETACHED BUNGALOW	Region 1				54.00	55.00	48.50	44.00	44.00	46.00
	2				47.50	48.00	42.50	38.50	38.50	40.00
	3				45.00	45.50	40.50	36.50	36.50	38.00
	4				42.50	43.50	38.50	34.50	34.50	36.00
	Typical Area ft²				1350	1200	800	1350	1200	800
TERRACED	Region 1	53.50	52.50	52.50	52.50	52.00	51.50	38.00	41.00	45.50
	2	47.00	46.00	46.00	46.00	45.50	45.50	33.50	36.00	40.00
	3	44.50	44.00	43.50	43.50	43.50	43.00	31.50	34.00	38.00
	4	42.50	41.50	41.50	41.50	41.00	41.00	30.00	32.50	36.00
	Typical Area ft²	1650	1350	1050	1350	1050	850	1650	1300	900

1. **London**
2. **South East and North West England** Bedfordshire, Berkshire, Buckinghamshire, Essex, Hampshire, Hertfordshire, Kent, Oxfordshire, Surrey, Sussex, Cheshire, Greater Manchester, Lancashire and Merseyside.
3. **Scotland, Wales and Northern England** All of Scotland and Wales and Cleveland, Cumbria, Durham, Northumberland, Tyne & Wear.
4. **East Anglia, Midlands, South West, Yorkshire & Humberside and Northern Ireland** All other counties.

1. This chart has been prepared by the Building Cost Information Service of the Royal Institution of Chartered Surveyors. It is impossible to cover all circumstances and, for instance, the chart is unsuitable for certain types of property including the following:–
   (a) Properties which are not built mainly of brick.
   (b) Properties with more than two storeys or with basements and cellars.
   (c) Flats, because there are wide differences in construction and responsibilities for shared parts.

normally paid annually by the Society and are charged to your mortgage account – although they can be paid in equal monthly instalments.

Providing that the sum insured represents the full rebuilding cost from the outset, under the Society's index-linked scheme, you are guaranteed that in the event of a valid claim the actual cost of repairing or rebuilding your property will be paid – even if it exceeds the sum insured. Another benefit is that no wear and tear deductions are made from the claim providing the property has been maintained in good repair.

Using the rebuilding cost table on page 17 you need to know four simple facts about your house:

1. Its location, according to the four regions tabulated.
2. Its age.
3. The type of property – eg detached, terraced, etc.
4. The area in square feet, measured in accordance with the illustration shown.

If you are buying a house to do up or are improving one you already own, you will need to do a reappraisal at the end of the project in order to make sure that your house is fully insured. It is important that you include all the improvements you have done and ensure that you are covered for the right amount – neither too little nor too much.

HOME BUILDINGS INSURANCE COVER

In addition to the actual structure of the house, your policy should cover you for the permanent fixtures and fittings – for example, built-in kitchen units, bathroom sanitaryare and fittings, built-in bedroom cupboards and interior decorations which form part of the buildings. Policies usually extend to include outbuildings such as garages, greenhouses and garden sheds, but there will be only limited cover for boundary walls, fences, gates, paths, swimming pools, where normal wear and tear has to be taken into account.

While most policies will cover you for damage due to fire, lightning, explosion, earthquake, and a host of other potential disasters such as subsidence, landslip, heave and falling trees, you will find that there are two specific points you must consider when

HOW TO MEASURE YOUR HOME

- Draw a rough plan of your house (see example below).

- If your house is not symmetrical – for example, if you have bay windows or an extension that does not run the length or width of your house (the red areas in our example) – ignore these for the time being so that you begin by measuring a symmetrical shape

- Using a metal tape measure or ruler, go outside and measure the **length** of your house – **to the nearest foot**. Jot down this measurement on your plan (28 feet in our example)

- Repeat the process to establish the width of your house (20 feet in our example)

- Multiply the length by the width to find the square footage of the symmetrical area

PLAN OF HOUSE

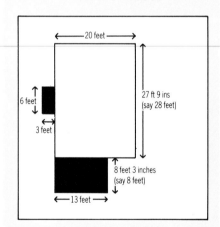

20 ft × 28 ft	=	560 sq.ft.
13 ft × 8 ft	=	104 sq.ft.
3 ft × 6 ft	=	18 sq.ft.
Total of ground floor: 682 sq.ft.		

- Measure any bay windows or extensions (the red areas in our example) and calculate the square footage in exactly the same way as for the symmetrical area

- Add the square footage of the two (red and blue) areas together to find the total square footage of the ground floor

- Measure other floors in the same manner, taking internal measurements and adding approximately 6 inches for the thickness of internal walls and 1 foot for the thickness of external walls

- Add the total area of ground floor and first floor together.

completing your proposal form. One is extensions to the policy and the other is exceptions and exclusions.

Among the usual sort of extensions are the following:

Alternative accommodation – if your home is so badly damaged by, for example, fire, that you will have to live in alternative accommodation. The cover will probably be expressed as a percentage of the sum insured.

Property Owners Liability – if, as the owner of your home, you are responsible for an injury to someone or for damage to their property, you will be covered both for the damages and the costs – usually to a specified limit which is often as much as £500,000 or more.

Underground Services – you could be covered for some disaster happening to the supply of gas, electricity, oil or water, as well as sewerage pipes, for accidental damage – but not for normal wear and tear.

Glass – indoors, windows and skylights, as well as being covered against breakage of wash basins, wcs and other such fixtures.

As with any legal document you will find that your policy does have limits and that there are exceptions and exclusions which should be carefully noted. Furthermore, you will find that for certain claims you will have to pay what is known as 'excess'. For example, for damage caused by storm, flood, or by malicious persons, you may have to pay an excess of £15 for each claim.

While your policy may cover you for subsidence, landslip or heave, you may have to pay out the first £500 of any claim running into thousands of pounds.

Some of the many common exclusions may include storm or flood damage caused to gates or fences, frost or sonic bangs, contamination by radioactivity from nuclear fuel, riot and malicious acts and war risks.

CONTENTS AND SECURITY

Every day a thousand homes in this country are burgled. That's one burglary every 90 seconds, with 9 out of 10 break-ins being through insecure windows and doors.

It is reckoned that 90 per cent of all burglaries are carried out by petty thieves or opportunists and such is the increase in burglary from domestic

property that you have a one-in-three chance of being burgled during your lifetime. It's not so much a question of *if* your home will be next, but *when*. Prevention, of course, is better than cure and in chapter 4 you will see some of the measures that can be taken to ensure that yours is a secure home. It is equally essential, of course, that the contents of your property are properly insured.

While no insurance policy can cover everything, and sometimes you have to bear some of the loss yourself, if you are really methodical with your approach you can make sure you obtain the best protection possible. You will find that proposal forms for insurance are very straightforward these days. Mostly it is a question of ticking boxes marked 'yes' or 'no' and making an assessment of the amount of cover required. There are two basic aspects to consider:

Contents and High Risk Items – you will need to list, room by room, all the items in your house. You will inevitably find that you have a great deal more than you first thought. Furthermore, the replacement cost due to inflation may also be much greater than you would guess. It will be important that you specify high-risk items such as your television set, audio and video equipment, jewellery, clocks, watches, cameras, fur coats, pictures, works of art, and so on. You may also think it sensible to be insured for any accidental damage – particularly if you have boisterous young children around.

Optional Extensions – such as 'All Risks' to cover your valuables, personal effects which you take with you when travelling around or going on holiday. Nowadays a freezer full of food can be expensive to replace, as can pedal cycles. It is also worth insuring your walletful of money and credit cards.

Nothing can make up for the personal sense of shock when your house has been violated by intruders, nor can you replace possessions prized mainly for their sentimental value, but at least insurance can make sure that you can recover the monetary value when disaster strikes. So if you are embarking on a home-improvement project which is going to add value to the structure of your property as well as to its contents, now is the time to make sure your overall insurance is up-to-date – with the premiums costed into the project.

THE OPTIONS

What is feasible within the space inside and outside your home?
What is allowable? These are the questions to answer before
you decide whether to move or improve.

Do you move or improve? That is the question many families have to answer at some time or another. Unless there is no real choice – when a change of job means moving to another part of the country or you simply don't like the house or the area in which you live – it makes sense to investigate and evaluate the possibilities of improving or enlarging your home as a practical alternative to the major upheaval which is involved with moving house.

If you consider such costs as removal, legal fees, agent's charges, stamp duty, and add to that the cost of refurbishing a new property, you will find you have a good four-figure sum which might well be better invested in a home improvement project. But what are the options? What is feasible? What is allowable? These and many other questions have to be answered before you can come to a firm decision.

While much will depend on the position of your property, the constraints of the existing structure and the application you have in mind, with most properties you will have at least one out of five basic options. You will either be able to go *up* with a roof conversion, or go *out* with an extension or perhaps go *down* with a basement conversion. You can carry out many different forms of internal alterations to the existing layout or external developments of the land surrounding the property. Which option, or as so often happens, which combination of options, is going to give you what you want, will depend entirely on your needs and what you can afford – providing it is allowable under the Town and Country Planning Acts.

TOWN & COUNTRY PLANNING ACTS

Town and country planning is essentially a matter of resolving the many needs and conflicts created by a society made up of authorities, statutory undertakers, developers, industrialists, house-owners, amenity groups, transport interests and individuals – all of whom may make demands on limited areas of land. The Local Planning Authority has to attempt to balance the often opposing views in order to arrive at a compatible scheme which meets most objections. Never an easy task and one which is always open to criticism.

Fortunately, most improvements and enlargements to private houses do not need planning consent because, under the General Development Order, every '*single family dwelling*' (unless the house or area is subject to a special order) may be enlarged by 70 cubic metres or 15 per cent of the volume of the original house up to a maximum of 115 cubic metres. This is subject to a number of conditions:

1. The addition must not exceed the height of the existing building.
2. The addition may not come in front of the forward-most point of the building where it fronts on to a highway.
3. No part of the extension which comes within 2 metres of the boundary of your property is more than 4 metres above the ground. This condition does not apply to extensions or alterations to the roof of the original house.
4. The extension will not result in more than half of the original garden area of the house being covered by buildings or structures.
5. The extension is not for occupation as a separate and independent dwelling.

However, if you live in a terraced house (including a house at the end of a terrace) the allowance is reduced to 50 cubic metres or 10 per cent of the cubic area up to the same maximum. This reduced allowance also applies if you live in an area of outstanding beauty or a conservation area.

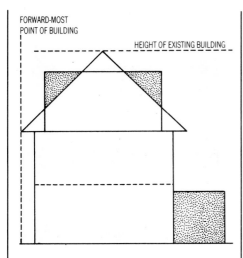

If your plans conform with these criteria you can go ahead with what is commonly known as 'permitted development' and no consent is required. There are, however, one or two points to take into account when making your assessment. Firstly, the 'original' means the house as first built, or as it stood on the 1st July 1948 if built before then. The allowance is once-and-for-all and any previous enlargement of the original house, even if carried out after an express grant of planning permission, counts against the allowance. So it is most important that you check whether, for example, an existing garage was built as part of the property or else added to since 1948 as this will have used up a considerable amount of your 'permitted development' allowance.

Secondly, the addition of a garage only counts as part of your allowance if it will come within 5 metres of your house.

There is one addition which may come in front of the building line and

PORCH EXTENSION

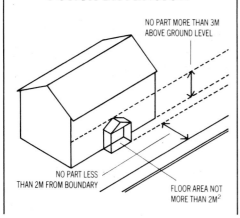

that is a porch. You will not need planning permission provided that all the following conditions are met:

1. The floor area is not more than 2 square metres.
2. No part of the porch is more than 3 metres above ground level.
3. No part of the porch is less than 3 metres from any boundary between your garden and the road or public footpath.

While a stable counts towards your 'permitted development' allowance, a garage sited more than 5 metres from the house counts as any other small structure which you are allowed to build within the boundary of your property, such as a shed, greenhouse, aviary, kennel, poultry house, summerhouse, swimming pool or sauna cabin. There are a number of provisos, as follows:

1. No part of the building should project beyond the forward-most part of any wall which fronts on to a highway. (A public footpath running alongside your property may count as a highway, so check with the planning authority on this.)
2. Such buildings must not exceed 4 metres in height if they have a ridge roof, or 3 metres otherwise.
3. The total area covered by the building must not be more than half the total ground area of the site – excluding the area covered by the house itself.
4. Such buildings must not require any new access to a trunk or classified road or necessitate the alteration of an existing access and will not obstruct the view of anyone using the highway used by vehicular traffic.
5. Such developments must not be contrary to any condition of an existing planning permission.

From the type of buildings mentioned, you will appreciate that the use must be for the personal enjoyment of the occupants of the house and must not be used for any commercial undertaking.

As can be seen, the 'permitted development' rule allows you to build a considerable amount in and around your property, but it also allows you to do one other thing. Unless it is a listed building or in a conservation area you are allowed to demolish any part of your house or an outbuilding. There are occasions when it makes sense to do so and there are other times when, by doing so, you can guarantee that your project will not require planning permission. This can be particularly important if there is a possibility that planning consent might well be refused.

For example, suppose you decided that you wanted a substantial kitchen extension to take the place of an outside lavatory at the rear of the building. The amount of cubic footage which the old building took up may be added to the overall size of the new extension.

On the other hand, the new development does not have to be directly related to the structure you wish to demolish. Suppose you required a loft conversion and it needed to have dormer windows facing to the front of the property and the overall size of the conversion was such that planning permission would have to be sought. In such circumstances, you could take down an existing garage (providing of course that it was not itself added as 'permitted development') so that the existing volume could then count towards the loft conversion.

Incidentally, the resulting hardstanding for the car would not require planning permission. In fact, at a later date you could always apply for planning permission for a new garage to be erected and since there had previously been one it would be more than likely that permission would be granted.

If you live in a conservation area or in a street whose character and appearance the authority is particularly anxious to protect, the local planning authority can serve what is known as an Article 4 direction on all householders affected. Such a notice will stop all your permitted development rights and you will have to apply for planning permission for everything you want to do.

It is also possible that the original planning permission granted for your house may have included a condition restricting or prohibiting some of the normal rights you might have had under the 'permitted development' rule. For

example, a new estate with open-plan front gardens might well have a planning condition prohibiting you from erecting any fences or constructing a hardstanding. Such a condition does not necessarily mean that the local planning authority will not allow you to do such work, but what it does mean is that you have to apply for planning permission. So, always check with the planning department.

Your 'permitted development' rights may also be affected by a restrictive covenant on your property or land. This can be enforced even if you have express planning permission to carry out the development, so always examine the deeds of your property and if necessary

Some lofts are bigger than others, but even small ones can have potential for extra storage or living space. A recent change in the Building Regulations means there is no longer a minimum height required for loft living rooms, so where previously dormer windows had to be fitted to give the necessary headroom, it may now be possible simply to install a Velux or similar window in the roof slope to achieve a worthwhile conversion.

consult your solicitor.

Some projects, of course, are of a scale that unavoidably calls for planning permission, but since the vast majority of home enlargement schemes can be catered for under the 'permitted development' rule let us look first at the options available before considering the need for going through the lengthy procedures and uncertainty associated with a planning application.

LOFT CONVERSION

Putting an empty loft into commission is an obvious way of gaining useful additional accommodation. Whereas a ground-floor extension eats into the garden, the loft conversion allows the house to be enlarged within itself without encroaching on any of the land around it. Most of the space already exists and it is only the dormer windows, if they are necessary, which are an extension to the property. This is therefore a form of home enlargement which can yield the greatest amount of space within the 'permitted development' rule.

Not every loft is suitable for conversion and much depends on the type of house, the roof structure, the layout of the rooms, the number of load-bearing walls and the means of access before you can determine the actual potential. The most important factor is the height of the existing roof and the length of the ridge as it sits either on a gable wall or at the point of two hip rafters. Consequently the ridge of the roof is either positioned 'gable-to-gable' or 'gable-to-hip' or 'hip-to-hip' and it's important that you recognise what category your house is.

GABLE-TO-GABLE
detached
semi-detached
mid-terrace

ELEVATION

PLAN

GABLE-TO-HIP
detached
semi-detached
end terrace

ELEVATION

PLAN

HIP-TO-HIP
detached
semi-detached

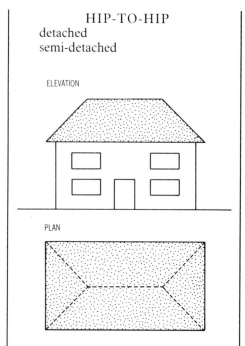

ELEVATION

PLAN

Many houses have additional bonnets or protrusions within the main roof, as well as having extensions to the rear, either at the same or a lower level. Struts and braces supporting the roof, chimneys and skylights with shafts to illuminate landings can also obstruct the roof from within. Indeed, you may well be confused the first time you climb into your loft as to how it can be converted – and you will certainly need professional advice before you do anything.

The first item to check is the height of the ridge as it is measured from underneath the ridge board to the top of the ceiling joists. Under the old regulations there was a specific requirement that a habitable room 'wholly or partly in the roof of the building' had to have a height of 'not less than 2.3 metres over an area of the floor of the room equal to not less than one half of the area of that room measured on a plane of 1.5 metres above the floor.' This provision, apart from being difficult for many a lay person to understand (let alone comply with!) stopped countless thousands of conversions from taking place.

However, under the Building Regulations 1985 this technical requirement for a mandatory floor-to-ceiling height has been dropped. You are now able to apply your own common sense when thinking of converting the wasted space in your loft. But there is a new regulation concerning the means of escape in case of fire. The details of this are considered in the next chapter.

Naturally, the higher the ridge the easier it is to convert the loft. The length of the ridge is also important in terms of establishing the amount of useable space you have available. Much depends on the way you interpret the word 'useable' in respect of the sloping rafters that naturally restrict headroom unless you strike out a dormer. Under the old regulations dormers were almost essential because of the mandatory floor-to-ceiling height – and, indeed, they will very often be required to provide access to a staircase.

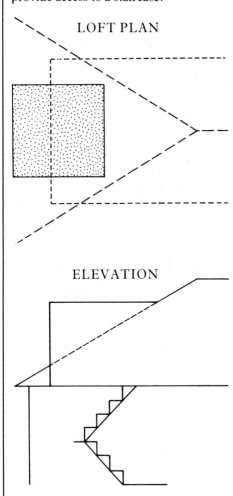

LOFT PLAN

ELEVATION

The new building regulations will allow for much more attractive loft conversions. This is because the way a dormer is normally constructed means that the structural beams have to run right across to the opposite roof slope and, as a result, you have to have a flat area of ceiling rather than open space right up to the apex of the roof. Without a dormer, you are able to use the full roof as part of your new room. If nothing else, this will create the feeling of a much more spacious room.

LOFT PLAN

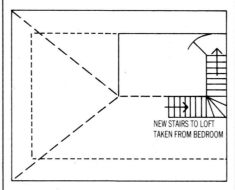

NEW STAIRS TO LOFT
TAKEN FROM BEDROOM

FIRST FLOOR PLAN

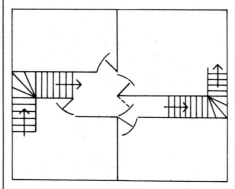

BASEMENT CONVERSION

If you can't go up perhaps you can go down. A surprising number of houses do have basements or voids suitable for converting into habitable rooms. The main problem is height, but unlike a roof conversion which cannot go beyond the ridge without planning permission, you can at least dig down your 'permitted development' allowance to achieve what you want.

Excavating out a basement is potentially hazardous, and it is essential that the foundations of the house are not undermined in any way. You will definitely need professional advice and a qualified structural engineer will have to satisfy the local authority that the work can be carried out safely as well as to a proper standard.

Windows must be incorporated, and of course it is necessary to 'tank' walls against the penetration of ground water, as well as making the new floor itself damp proof. You will need the services of a specialist contractor for the underpinning of the foundations and this is likely to be an expensive exercise. Brickwork is often of poor quality and this can mean structural complications during the alterations. And with the new foundations at a different level to the neighbouring buildings, there can also be problems of differential settlement.

Other important aspects of a basement conversion include dealing with the drainage, where making connections to the sewer could be difficult owing to the low level of the basement. The new room must also have a proper level of fire resistance from the upper floors, because the house will become a three-storey building.

Many town houses with basements have an area to the front with steps going down to an external door. This provides the opportunity to create a totally self-contained flat – especially if the garden to the rear can be excavated and 'pushed back' so that a patio door can be installed to bring in light and air from a subterranean terrace. If nothing else, a basement can yield an extremely useful utility room, workshop or games room for the family.

With the restrictions lifted on the mandatory floor-to-ceiling height for habitable rooms, there are now many more basements which can be put into commission. It is certainly an option worth considering if you are fortunate enough to have one.

EXTENDING OUTWARDS

Unlike a conversion of existing space which is mainly within the house, an extension is mostly new building works added to the property. As such, the extension can either be a purpose-built addition on one or more levels or else a prefabricated structure, such as a conservatory or garage.

Most houses have some land either to the front, side or rear on which it might be possible to build an extension of one or more storeys.

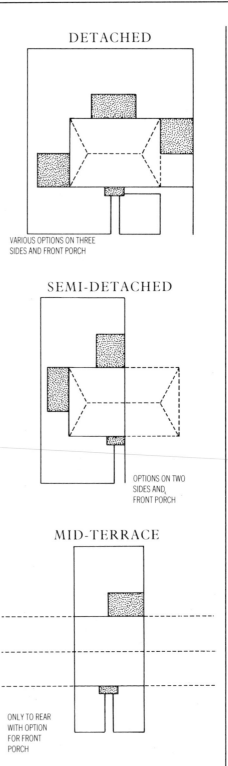

DETACHED

VARIOUS OPTIONS ON THREE SIDES AND FRONT PORCH

SEMI-DETACHED

OPTIONS ON TWO SIDES AND FRONT PORCH

MID-TERRACE

ONLY TO REAR WITH OPTION FOR FRONT PORCH

With a basement it is quite feasible to excavate out the area (putting in a retaining wall to hold the earth back) to create space for an extension to be built outwards. Such extensions usually consist of a high proportion of glass to bring the light down into the subterranean space. But most extensions are built at ground level either to the rear or possibly the sides of the property either as rooms in their own right or, more often, as enlargements to existing rooms such as kitchens and living areas.

Such an extension may have either a pitched or a flat roof. While a pitched roof does help to make the extension look less 'box-like', a flat roof may allow for a marginally bigger living space when it comes to totting up the cubic footage allowance under the 'permitted development' rule.

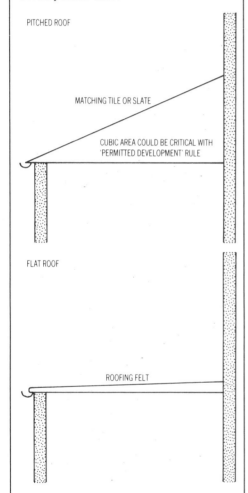

PITCHED ROOF

MATCHING TILE OR SLATE

CUBIC AREA COULD BE CRITICAL WITH 'PERMITTED DEVELOPMENT' RULE

FLAT ROOF

ROOFING FELT

Creating an additional living room is a popular project, particularly with patio doors or french windows leading on to the garden. Extending and redesigning the whole kitchen to make a larger room in which to take meals – perhaps freeing the existing dining room for use as a study on an everyday basis – is another popular scheme.

An extension by the side of a kitchen can provide a well-equipped utility room for a washing machine and deep freeze, as well as extra space for parking

wellingtons, raincoats and the like.

When building a ground extension with a flat roof, it is certainly worth considering using the roof as a terrace approached from one of the rooms on the first floor. This way you are able to reclaim the slice of garden you had to use and it makes an attractive amenity for the bedroom above. Of course you can build on at both ground and first-floor level and create, perhaps, an en suite bathroom for the bedroom concerned.

You can also consider a partial first-floor addition above a ground-floor extension, to create a balcony. Or you might even cantilever out a balcony to form part of a covered way beneath.

Another logical place to create more living space is to build up over an attached garage. You have to be sure that the garage has sufficiently strong foundations and walls to carry the additional load, as well as making sure that the garage is brought up to the fire standard required. Some houses have a garage built into the main structure with a sloping roof over it. In this case it is more of a question of striking out a dormer or, if there is enough room, putting in roof windows, rather than actually building up.

With any form of purpose-built extension the architect or building surveyor does have wide scope for making the addition blend in well with the house. However, while it is not possible to achieve the same degree of flexibility with a prefabricated structure, there are certainly some very advanced products available to help you create additional living space.

A simple extension can provide not only additional living space, but the pleasures of year-round gardening into the bargain.

A conservatory or a sun lounge is a very popular form of prefabricated extension and, in the main, they are very simple to erect – on a DIY basis or through a service provided by the manufacturer. Some of the most common prefabricated units sold are front porches and, in fact, this is the only form of extension which can come to the front of the house beyond the building line, as part of your permitted development allowance.

INTERNAL ALTERATIONS

Since all the older properties in this country were built for a different age and manner of living, most need at least some form of alterations to existing layout to cope with today's lifestyle.

For example, a large bedroom in a Victorian house might well become two smaller bedrooms or, perhaps, produce an en suite bathroom. Two small back and front living rooms in an Edwardian terrace might have the dividing wall knocked through to make a much bigger room. The understairs cupboard of a pre-war suburban house could probably yield a valuable cloakroom. An old scullery off a kitchen could be transformed into a useful utility room. There are a mass of options which can be considered.

Great numbers of houses in this country were built with an outside lavatory – and very often a coal store next to it – attached to the rear of the property. It is a relatively easy alteration to make this part of the main house. By breaking through the external wall of the house and bricking up the doors of the outbuildings, you can put the space to a number of very good uses.

Sliding patio doors bring a remarkable sense of spaciousness to any room, as well as a panoramic view of the great outdoors.

In fact, with 'outshoots' of a property it may be more expedient to demolish the structure and incorporate the value of the cubic footage as part of an overall – much better designed – extension to the house. While this might very well cost more, it should also add real value to the property.

Internal alterations tend to involve either breaking through or taking down an existing wall, which must be done at no risk to the structural stability of the house. Or, it is a question of building 'stud' walls to produce enclosures or sub-divisions of rooms. While planning permission will not be required, this sort of work will inevitably mean that plans have to be deposited with the local authority for building control approval.

Perhaps the most common internal alteration is to take out an existing window and insert a patio door. Very often this means making a much wider opening and, while you might not think it much of a structural alteration, it is something that has to be carried out carefully for the integrity of the building to be maintained. Patio doors bring a lot of light and air into the room and, mostly, open directly on to the garden – the careful development of which can add lasting value to the property.

EXTERNAL DEVELOPMENTS

There are many ways in which the surrounding land of a property can be developed and improved. Under 'permitted development' rights half the garden area may be covered with buildings before any planning consent is required – which should be more than enough for most people.

Nowadays, high land prices tend to mean new houses have the minimum amount of garden a property developer considers he can get away with. So homes on a new estate will commonly have a pocket handkerchief at the front and a tablecloth at the back! However, the boundaries of older properties are sometimes more generous, often unusual in shape, much more matured and offering considerable scope for landscaping.

There are several aspects under the Town & Country Planning Acts which need to be noted before planning anything. Starting with the boundary of your property, you may not build a wall

Under 'permitted development' rights, half the garden area may be covered by outbuildings without planning consent. So you can, within certain height restrictions, put up a greenhouse, potting shed or other structure with no problem. Such buildings are not subject to building control, and there are many good prefabricated structures that can be built as a DIY project.

or fence more than a metre high where it runs along an adjoining highway used by vehicular traffic. Elsewhere, a fence or wall can be 2 metres high. However, it is worth noting that if you want to go higher than that there is no planning control over hedges.

CHANGING ACCESS

In most cases you will need planning permission to construct a means of access, such as a path or driveway, to the road. However, if the access is to an unclassified road and is needed in connection with a structure you are entitled to build on your property, you will not require planning permission. Nevertheless, you should seek highway authority consent if your means of access involves the crossing of any footpath or verge of the road. The district council or London borough council will be able to tell you whether a particular road in their area is unclassified, classified or a trunk road, and they will also tell you which is the appropriate highway authority.

If you are fortunate enough to have some fine trees in your garden, it is important to check whether any of them

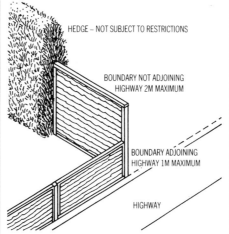

HEDGE – NOT SUBJECT TO RESTRICTIONS

BOUNDARY NOT ADJOINING HIGHWAY 2M MAXIMUM

BOUNDARY ADJOINING HIGHWAY 1M MAXIMUM

HIGHWAY

are protected by a Tree Preservation Order (TPO) which prevents you either felling or lopping them. If you live in a conservation area you should also notify the local authority before felling or lopping any trees and, if in doubt it is important to check with the planning department.

You do not need planning permission to install a central heating oil tank in your garden. But if, like many people, you decide to change from oil to gas and want to install a domestic L P G tank, you will need permission.

Some three million homes still have no access to natural gas, but the Calor bulk-delivery system presents a useful alternative. Curiously, while planning permission is not required for an oil tank in your garden, you do need consent for a domestic LPG tank.

To park a caravan or boat in your drive or garden, planning permission is not required if either are used for your own enjoyment and simply parked there when not in use. A caravan parked in the garden may be used by members of your own household, but cannot be used as an independent dwelling without planning permission. Some authorities have special local powers to prohibit the parking of caravans and boats in front gardens and if there is any doubt you should check with your local planning department. You will not need permission to construct a hardstanding – as long as the vehicle is not for trade or hire.

If you wish to install a swimming pool and to build a sauna cabin or summer house to go with it, planning permission will not be needed providing your garden is of a size that allows you to do so. The same goes for greenhouses, sheds and small buildings to house animals 'kept for the domestic needs or the personal enjoyment of the occupants of the house' – for example rabbit hutches would be included in this category.

There is certainly much that you can do to develop the garden and surrounding area of your house and as long as you don't go overboard, the extra amenities may well add value to your property. For a really major improvement that is not feasible under the 'permitted development' rule, however, you will have to go through the complete procedure for getting planning permission.

PLANNING PERMISSION

If your project needs planning permission, the very first thing to do is to go to the planning department of your district council or London borough and collect the necessary application form. Ask to see one of the Planning Officers, who will be able to help you with any queries on completing the form as well as giving an informal view on whether or not what you have in mind is likely to be acceptable.

The Planning Officer will also tell you what fee you will have to pay for the submission of a planning application to enlarge, alter, improve or extend an existing dwelling house. When the fees were introduced in April 1981 the rate was £20; it had risen to £27 by August 1985 and may well have gone up marginally more by the time you make your application.

Procedures differ slightly from one authority to another, but most planning committees listen carefully to what their officers have to say and if a proposed scheme is recommended by the planning department it will have a much greater chance of getting through than if it is not. The basic principle adopted by local planning authorities is that householders should be free to carry out whatever development or improvement to their own property they wish, unless there is a good planning reason for refusing permission.

Most applications are successful, but often require slight modifications or conditions to overcome potential objections. It is only reasonable that the local planning authority is concerned to see that the general amenities of the area are not affected by individual developments.

NEIGHBOURLY INTEREST

If what you are proposing is going to be a real eyesore, your application may well be refused – and quite rightly! Your neighbours can certainly make representations to the council about your application, and the Planning Officer is more than likely to discuss it with them in any case. So do discuss your ideas with your neighbours and seek their agreement before you start. In doing so, bear in mind that the purpose of planning control is to safeguard the public interest and not to protect the private interest of one person against another. The planning authority must confine itself to objections which have to do with planning matters and nothing else.

Planning Committees are made up of lay people and, whilst they more often than not heed the advice of the professionals in the planning department, their decisions are reached in the usual democratic fashion. Since local councillors come in different political colours one authority's views may differ substantially from another, so their pronouncements can always be challenged on appeal to the Secretary of State for the Environment. The Department of the Environment formulates national policy and every so often it reviews various aspects of the Planning Acts to keep them in line with the nation's needs.

It is always necessary to apply for planning permission for a 'change of use' of a property. However, planning permission is not usually needed if the character and use of the building remain essentially residential.

For example, if you wish to use part of your home as bedsitter or for bed and breakfast accommodation you are unlikely to need permission. Nor are you likely to need permission to use a room as your personal office or for a business such as hairdressing, dressmaking, music teaching or tuition.

A change in character or use will probably arise if the answer to any of the following questions is yes:

Will your home cease to be used substantially as a private residence?
Will any part of your home no longer be used for private residential purposes?
Will the proposed business involve any activities unusual in a residential area?
Will your business disturb your neighbours at unreasonable hours or be the source of loud noise or strong smells?

If you have any doubts at all, it is advisable to check with your local authority about the Use Classes Order under the Town & Country Planning Acts.

DON'T RISK IT

If you go ahead with a project which requires planning consent, without first applying, you could find yourself in serious trouble. The local authority would have two options. Either it might regularise the situation by requiring you to submit an application for permission and, if what you have done is reasonable, grant it. Or, it would have the power to serve an enforcement notice on you to restore the property to its original condition before you carried out the work.

Such an order could be costly indeed! So, however confident you might be that a major project can be considered a 'permitted development' do remember that the onus is very much on you to prove the point. Always try and get written agreement from the planning department to confirm that your interpretation of just what is permissible is in fact a correct one. For a substantial scheme it is probably best to obtain the services of a professional advisor to act for you.

GETTING IT DONE

Today's building regulations are more flexible than ever and certain home improvements are now exempt altogether. But for any substantial improvement project you need professional advice, and guaranteed standards of work and workmanship from your builder.

For any substantial home improvement project, professional advice makes sense. Quite apart from the design side, the supervision of your project by an architect or chartered surveyor could well save you from the potentially disastrous consequences of bad building work.

Given the financial resources and a clear idea of the options open, you are now in a position to start your project. If what you have in mind is a substantial scheme involving structural alterations and building works, you should consider taking on a qualified professional to act on your behalf. Even if you intend to do as much of the work as you can yourself, you will probably need expert advice if you are to avoid major pitfalls along the way.

Who you should use depends very largely on the type of work involved. Whoever he or she is (for the purpose of simplicity – with no sexism intended – I will refer just to the male gender!) you must be sure he is both competent and able to accept full responsibility for his work. Many a technician or draughtsman can produce a set of drawings, but just how qualified are they to translate them into a properly executed, finished construction? One question which usually sorts out the qualified professional from the rest is: 'Do you have indemnity insurance for negligence?' The two professionals who can certainly answer that question in the affirmative are an architect or a chartered building surveyor.

Both are eminently qualified when it comes to dealing with small domestic properties. It is only when considering, perhaps, the design of a whole estate of houses or complete urban renewal scheme that one profession rather than the other tends to be chosen. What matters is that you should use one or the other, rather than some unqualified designer or other practitioner with dubious or inappropriate qualifications.

THE ARCHITECT

Although the word *architect* is freely used to describe a designer of buildings or one who prepares plans and superintends construction, its professional use is in fact protected by Act of Parliament. The only person who can call himself an architect is one who has qualified by examination and is registered with the Architects' Registration Council of the United Kingdom.

The vast majority of architects, once registered, become members of the Royal Institute of British Architects and have the letters RIBA after their name. To qualify for corporate membership of the RIBA and for registration under the Architects' (Registration) Act 1931 candidates have to go through a lengthy and comprehensive training of at least seven years before they can put 'architect' against their name.

Having qualified as a member of the RIBA, architects are governed by the Charters, Byelaws and Codes of Professional Conduct of the Royal Institute, which determine their relationships with the public and their professional colleagues. Very obviously, any architect has to be dedicated to go through all the necessary training and, considering the tremendous competition from totally unqualified people, it is not all that easy to practise in accordance with the very strict rules. Unhappily, standards are today being eroded in the name of liberation (architects are now, for example, allowed to advertise), while the profession could serve its own interests – and those of the public – better by pressing for more severe measures against those who try falsely to pass themselves off as qualified people.

The trouble is that while the term architect is protected by law, anyone can set themselves up as a designer offering an 'architectural service' or use any other 'architectural' sounding name. As a result many members of the public who know nothing of what it actually means to gain the professional qualification of an *architect* can easily be fooled by an imposing letterhead or an attractively worded advertisement for services. The fact that architects' practices may now advertise can only help to confuse the situation further.

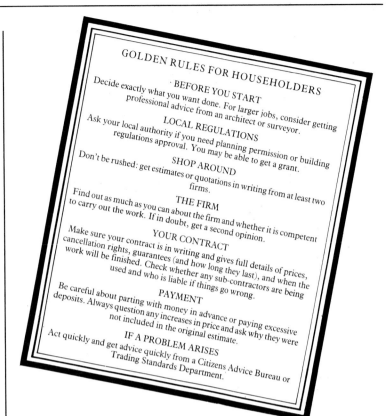

GOLDEN RULES FOR HOUSEHOLDERS

BEFORE YOU START
Decide exactly what you want done. For larger jobs, consider getting professional advice from an architect or surveyor.

LOCAL REGULATIONS
Ask your local authority if you need planning permission or building regulations approval. You may be able to get a grant.

SHOP AROUND
Don't be rushed: get estimates or quotations in writing from at least two firms.

THE FIRM
Find out as much as you can about the firm and whether it is competent to carry out the work. If in doubt, get a second opinion.

YOUR CONTRACT
Make sure your contract is in writing and gives full details of prices, cancellation rights, guarantees (and how long they last), and when the work will be finished. Check whether any sub-contractors are being used and who is liable if things go wrong.

PAYMENT
Be careful about parting with money in advance or paying excessive deposits. Always question any increases in price and ask why they were not included in the original estimate.

IF A PROBLEM ARISES
Act quickly and get advice quickly from a Citizens Advice Bureau or Trading Standards Department.

To help you choose an architect, the RIBA has a *Client's Advisory Service* which can put you in touch with two or three local practices in your area. Furthermore, if you can take the time to visit their offices at 66 Portland Place, London W1 you can peruse the various files in order to see examples of the type of work a particular practice has done. It is, naturally, important to select an architect with whom you feel you can work. You need to find someone who can appreciate that, although your home extension may not, in the scale of things, be a particularly large scheme for him, it is a vitally important project to you, in which you want to be sure everything will run smoothly – and to budget.

THE CHARTERED BUILDING SURVEYOR

Just as the use of the term architect is governed by Act of Parliament, so is the word 'chartered' as it is applied to a surveyor protected by Royal Charter. The chartered building surveyor is qualified by examination in the construction and economics of buildings old and new and will be fully conversant with all aspects of town planning and building regulation matters. He will be well qualified to draw up the plans, and to prepare specifications and estimates for home-improvement work, as well as

All qualified chartered surveyors are members of the Royal Institution of Chartered Surveyors. A 'surveyor' without this membership will probably not be qualified to advise you.

The vast majority of architects belong to the Royal Institute of British Architects: look for the designatory letters after their names. While the word architect is protected by law, anyone can offer an 'architectural service' – so take care!

carrying out site supervision and the management of building contracts.

In much the same way as an architect suffers the unqualified rivalry of 'architectural' consultants and the like, so too does the chartered surveyor face a large measure of competition from people describing themselves as plain 'surveyor'. Unlike the architect who may or may not belong to the RIBA, all chartered surveyors do have to be members of the Royal Institution of Chartered Surveyors. This means they will have the designatory letters ARICS or FRICS after their name. Once again, if you write to the RICS at 12 Great George Street, Parliament Square, London SW1 you can request the names of local practices in your area and be able to make a choice.

NEGOTIABLE FEES

All architects used to charge the same basic fees, based on a set of standard, mandatory figures prepared by the RIBA, but a new system has now been developed which offers 'greater flexibility to both architect and client.' This simply means that the fee is open to negotiation. However, their code of Professional Conduct requires architects to define the terms of an appointment, including the scope of the work, the allocation of responsibilities and any limitation of liability, as well as the fee basis before accepting a commission. Chartered surveyors operate in much the same fashion.

For a full supervising brief, if you allow between 10 and 15 per cent you won't be far out. Whatever the actual figure is, it represents a very sound investment which is quite likely to be recouped simply through saving the money which might well be lost through the unfettered performance of some builders! Bear in mind, too, that if you accept the services of an unqualified practitioner at a fee of a few percentage points less, you will be sacrificing the peace of mind which goes with using a properly qualified person carrying full indemnity insurance.

Both the RIBA and RICS have professional indemnity insurance schemes for their members and it is important to check that the practice you are intending to use is properly covered. It is not unknown for an architect or

surveyor who is employed by a firm to accept individual, private commissions on his own. In which case, it is even more important that you establish the position of professional indemnity before you go ahead.

For a very straightforward project or renovation scheme, you may feel that you need an architect or surveyor simply to draw up the plans and specification and submit them for planning permission and building control – leaving you to negotiate and supervise the work with the builder. In such circumstances, you can agree a straight fee, usually charged on a time basis.

FINDING A BUILDER

Trying to find a good and reliable builder can be the trickiest part of any home improvement project. Even when you do find a really first-class contractor the chances are the firm will have a very full order book. But good builders *do* exist and it is worth spending considerable time trying to find one.

It is certainly true that the building industry abounds with 'cowboys' (the term apparently originated in America where out-of-work ranch hands used to drift into the towns and cities to find casual labour on building sites) and, as a result, it is not so surprising that this industry alone contributes about 20 per cent of all the bankruptcies in Britain. The size of the problem can be seen from the fact that the Office of Fair Trading receives around 40,000 complaints a year. So it is worth heeding the OFT's seven golden rules when initiating a home-improvement project (on page 33).

To help combat the problem both the building federations now run consumer protection schemes and it makes good sense to take advantage of them. However, one of the schemes does have the drawback of preventing you using a professional advisor throughout the course of the contract, while the other is subscribed to by so few of its membership that you may have difficulty in locating a firm within your immediate area.

Building Employers Confederation

The Building Employers Confederation (BEC) is the leading builders' organisation in this country. It has around 10,000 members, including multi-national contrators, specialist contractors and local builders. While the federation's guarantee scheme is mandatory on all its members, it only applies in reality to about two thirds of the total, as most of the very large firms do not do small domestic work.

The BEC regard their scheme as a double assurance to clients. This is because the confederation consider that choosing one of their members in the first place means you can be confident you are using a firm which operates in accordance with good practice. Secondly, the firm has to offer you the *BEC Guarantee Scheme* for all work in the range £500 to £25,000. For a minimum fee of £20 or 1 per cent of the contract price, you receive a guarantee, underwritten by the Norwich Union, that if the BEC member does not carry out his contract satisfactorily the job will be completed on the terms originally agreed. However there is a major proviso: any additional cost in having the work rectified will be up to a maximum of £5,000.

SPECIAL CONDITION

Perhaps the greatest drawback of the scheme is that it only applies if you are dealing direct with one of the members and have not engaged an architect, surveyor or other qualified professional to act for you while the work is being done. In other words, you can engage a professional advisor to draw up the plans and specification and tender the work out, but if you want the benefits of the BEC Guarantee Scheme then your professional advisor may not act as the supervising officer during the course of the contract.

The whole scheme has been well conceived. There is a conciliation service if any disagreement arises between you and the builder and if such a dispute cannot be resolved, then there is an arbitration service to decide matters. The guarantee covers any disputes arising out of your contract while the work is being carried out and for a period of six months after the member tells you that the work is completed – that is, when it is ready for you to take the work over. The scheme also extends for a period of two years from the end of the defects-liability

period to cover any defects which affect the structural function of the property for which the member has a responsibility under the contract.

Federation of Master Builders

The Federation of Master Builders (FMB) has some 20,000 members and the consumer protection scheme it runs is a voluntary one. Known as the federation's *Warranty Scheme*, only about 1,000 members subscribe to it, but those that do have to offer the scheme to all their prospective clients.

With a higher ceiling of £35,000, the scheme also pays up to a higher figure of £7,000 for any proven additional costs to complete a contract if the member goes into liquidation while the work is in progress. The warranty also continues for two years after the work has been completed, with the major advantage over the BEC scheme that there is no condition barring you from employing a professional to supervise the contract.

The real benefit of both these schemes is the protection you receive against the consequences of the builder going bust halfway through the work. Of all the potential hazards this is probably the worst – especially if you have in any way overpaid for the work done or, most commonly, it is going to cost a great deal more to put the original work right as part of completing the original contract. However good an architect or surveyor may be at ensuring that the quality of work meets his specification he cannot – at the outset of a contract – guarantee the financial stability of the building firm employed.

It is all too easy for a small building firm to get into financial difficulties. Many of them are under-capitalised and may get overstretched by taking on too many jobs at one time. There are countless plausible reasons why their finances go awry and there are certainly times when it is their clients' fault as much as their own! Of course, it doesn't matter *why* the firm goes into liquidation; it is the fact that it has and what the consequences are for you that is all-important. The 1 per cent of contract price for the insurance premium seems very good value in the circumstances.

The most important thing with any building contract is to make sure you only pay for work done. If you have engaged an architect or surveyor he will

The Federation of Master Builders has some 20,000 members – look for the symbol on their business paper and advertisements. But only about 1,000 of the members offer the federation's warranties – symbolised by the Warranty Shield.

ensure that the certificates he issues are for just that. But if you are supervising the work yourself, you must ensure that the work done does conform exactly with your agreed terms before you sign a cheque. If the money is being paid in stages directly by the building society, you will be protected by the society's valuer. He will inspect the work at each stage and only authorise payment if it has been properly completed.

EMPLOYING A BUILDER YOURSELF

If, having had the plans and the specification drawn up, you intend to employ the builder yourself, write to both the federations and get the names of local members in your area. In the case of the Federation of Master Builders, you should state clearly that you want only members who can offer the Warranty Scheme. You may well know some of the names and perhaps have seen their sign boards outside houses in your area. Ask friends and neighbours whether they know any of the names.

Then start telephoning to get appointments for your shortlist of firms to come and see you and discuss your project. Since with smaller firms the principal is probably out on site during the day, it is best to telephone either at lunchtime – when he may have popped back to the office – or in the late afternoon/early evening. Then, with your plans and specification draw up a list of questions, which might include some of the following:

How long has the firm been established?

How experienced is the firm in this type of work?

Can you have some current references and may you see some of their work?

Can you have the name of their bankers in order to obtain an inter-bank reference through yours, to assure yourself of their financial stability?

Does the firm employ all its own labour?

Does the firm subcontract any of the work – if so what and to whom and how long has the firm known them?

Will the firm take full responsibility for any subcontract work – and all the payments concerned?

What is the method of stage payments and will you only be invoiced for work done?

Does the firm carry third party and employer's liability and can you see a valid insurance certificate before the work is started?

Will the contract be subject to a 6-month maintenance period?

Can you register the contract with the guarantee or warranty scheme?

No decent firm will mind you asking such questions. They will understand your reasons and respect you for being cautious and businesslike. By the same token, the firm will probably want to know one or two things about you, so be prepared to answer such questions as:

Do you have direct funds or will money be released in stage payments by the building society?

Have you got planning permission and is it part of his contract to submit for building control?

Will his men be able to start at 8.00 am and finish late, if need be?

What access has he got to the property and where can he store materials?

These are but some of the many questions which will be raised on both sides and you should, with the firm to whom you finally award the contract, confirm as many points in writing as you can – at the outset.

BUILDING CONTROL

If your project involves the extension of a building, the material alteration of it or a change of use, the work will have to be carried out in accordance with the Building Regulations. Even if you are employing a professional advisor or are letting the builder deal with all the building control matters, it is as well for you to understand what the procedures are. It is the building's owner, in the end, who is ultimately responsible for seeing that the property conforms with the law.

On the 11th November 1985 new building regulations, in a revised form, came into force. Known as the Building Regulations 1985, they were made under the enabling powers in a consolidating Building Act of 1984. They are based on those laid down in the Building Regulations of 1976, but have been put into a shorter form and presented in a much more readily understood fashion. They are now more flexible in application and should be easier to amend where necessary.

The Building Regulations 1985 consist of 14 documents comprising:

The manual
Means of escape in case of fire
Material and workmanship

These are supported by 11 'Approved Documents' marked A – L as follows:

A – Structure
B – Fire
C – Site preparation
D – Toxic substances
E – Sound
F – Ventilation
G – Hygiene
H – Drainage, waste disposal
J – Heat producing appliances
K – Stairways, ramps and guards
L – Conservation of fuel and power

The Manual and the following two documents are mandatory, while the remaining 11 Approved Documents have been approved by the Secretary of State as practical guidance to meeting the requirements of the Regulations. There is no obligation to adopt any particular solution in the 11 documents if you prefer to meet the requirement in some other way. However, if a contravention of a requirement is alleged, and you have followed the guidance in one of the Approved Documents, that will be evidence 'tending to show that you have complied with the regulations'. If you have not followed the guidance, that will be evidence 'tending to show you have not complied' and it will be up to you to demonstrate by other means that you have followed the Regulations.

The regulations apply to the majority of building operations, including drainage and fittings, heating appliances, cavity-wall filling and underpinning. They also apply where a material change of use to an existing building is intended. Together with associated legislation, codes of practice and other rules, they lay down minimum safety and health standards to ensure that the building is structurally sound, weathertight, adequately drained and has satisfactory services.

Certain buildings are exempt from the regulations and the ones concerning home improvement are as follows:

The extension of a building by

the addition at ground level of a greenhouse, conservatory, porch, covered yard or covered way, as well as a carport which is open on at least two sides. However, the floor area of any of these extensions must not exceed 30 square metres.

A detached building having a floor area which does not exceed 30 square metres which contains no sleeping accommodation and is either situated more than 1 metre from the boundary or is a single storey building constructed wholly of non-combustible material.

A detached building designed and intended to shelter people from the effects of nuclear, chemical or conventional weapons and not used for·any other purpose. This, too, must have a floor area that does not exceed 30 square metres and the excavation of the building may not be closer to any exposed part of another building than the distance equal to the depth of the excavation plus 1 metre.

Some of the requirements of earlier regulations have now been removed. There is no minimum ceiling height for a habitable room, there is no need for ventilation to some lobbies, nor is there any need to have a zone of open space outside windows of habitable rooms. There is also a reduction in the detail requirements for stairways and in the

Reroofing is a skilled business which calls for a professional contractor fully equipped for the job.

requirements for non-combustible materials. There is the introduction of a new term 'limited combustibility' – namely materials which do not contribute to risk in case of fire.

Another new term 'material alteration' has replaced the previous 'structural alteration' which had lead to considerable dispute in the past. Material alteration is defined as, (a) work which would *adversely affect* the existing building in relation to its compliance with regulations concerning structural stability, means of escape or the internal or external fire-spread requirement, (b) the insertion of insulation into cavity walls, and (c) the underpinning of a building.

Provision was made in the Building Act 1984 for the Secretary of State for the Environment (and bodies he will designate for the purpose) to appoint 'Approved Inspectors' who may certify and supervise work under the building regulations. This system will allow any person intending to carry out building work an alternative to the control service run by the local authority. However, to date only the National Housebuilding Council (NHBC Building Control Services Ltd) has been appointed as an 'Approved Inspector' to operate in the low-rise, new housing field. Building control regulation in the great majority of cases therefore remains in the hands of local authorities for the time being.

HOW TO APPLY

There are two different ways of applying to the local authority for approval of building work under the regulations. The homeowner can either deposit 'full plans', namely two copies of detailed plans of the work, or give a 'building notice', which is a simple statement providing information concerning the work – sometimes with a 1-1250 scale site plan. The advantages or otherwise of each procedure should be considered before you apply.

With the full plans procedure, deposited plans must be passed or rejected by the local authority within 5 weeks, or, by agreement, within 2 months from the date of deposit. They can be rejected if they are defective because, for example, they fail to give information, or they show a contravention of the regulations.

Deposited plans may be approved conditionally if so requested or agreed by the applicant. They may also be accompanied by an Approved Plan certificate to show that they have been checked for compliance with the requirements for structural stability and energy conservation, in which case the local authority *cannot* reject the plans on grounds relating to such requirements. Where work on site conforms with the Approved Plans it gives the homeowner useful protection from an enforcement action by the local authority to remove or alter that work.

BUILDING NOTICE

The alternative procedure of giving a Building Notice requires minimal information to be given to the local authority in order to identify the property, the nature of the work and the opportunity to consider any affect the proposals might have related to linked powers or any local acts. In the case of a home extension, a plan to a scale of not less than 1:1250 is required to give additional information on building size, position and property boundaries, as well as the number of storeys in the building and the width and position of any adjoining streets.

The Building notice option relies on the inspection of work on site by the local authority and depends upon the owner's or his builder's knowledge and a clear understanding of the requirements of the regulations to ensure the work complies. The protection of having Approved Plans is not available because neither the building notice nor accompanying plans are treated as having been deposited. Therefore, the local authority can require work to be altered if it does not comply with the regulations.

Once the full plans or a building notice have been deposited, work may start on site provided the proper notice is given to the local authority of the commencement and, subsequently, notices are given for inspection at certain stages of the construction. You need to give 48 hours notice of the commencement of work and only 24 hours notice for the covering up of any foundation, excavation, and damproof course, or any concrete or other oversite material, or any drain or private sewer.

Notice is also required for the laying of a drain or private sewer, or haunching or back-filling the trench not more than 7 days after such work is carried out. Notification of the completion of the building work also has to be given not more than 7 days after the event.

There can be severe penalties for not observing the requirements of the regulations and enforcement powers are given to the local authority to require the removal or alteration of offending work. In fact, under the Building Act 1984, if a person contravenes any provision contained in building regulations he is liable, on summary conviction, to a substantial fine and a further fine not exceeding £50 for each day on which the default continues after he is convicted.

PRODUCT SELECTION

While all the elements of the building work will have been specified at the design stage, many of the 'finishing' items will be down to you to choose. Supposing for example you are having a second bathroom installed, you will obviously want to choose the sanitaryware yourself. You need to select the type of fittings, as well as accessories such as tiles, mirrors, cabinets and so on. You will wish to decide on the type of flooring you intend to use. If you are having a shower installed you will want to know what type, what sort of shower curtain or enclosure. In fact, there will be quite a number of items you should decide on personally – so where do you start?

First of all, make sure that your contract with the builder is absolutely clear as to which items you are obtaining and which he is supplying. You should set up a filing system for all the sales leaflets, brochures and catalogues you will accumulate as part of your selection process. Once you have narrowed down your options, you can visit a shortlist of stockists to see some of the items before you make your final decision.

The hard-hitting advertising on televison for American-style discount stores will no doubt catch your eye and the move by retailers like Tesco, Woolworths, Sainsburys and W H Smith into the booming field of home improvements means that you will probably start with the High Street.

However, the traditional middleman between the manufacturer and the user has long been the builders' merchant. For what is known as the 'heavy side' this is still very much so, because the user is the builder and he is the person buying the bulk materials that make up the structure. But on the 'light side' which includes such items as sanitaryware, kitchen units, showers, and radiators the householder as the end user, is much more concerned than ever before to choose exactly what he or she wants – and at the best price.

The trend is for homeowners to exclude such items from the specification and purchase the products direct for the builder to install. This buy-it-yourself concept has certain cash-flow advantages for the builder, but it has had its drawbacks for the traditional buiilders' merchant. Whereas places like B & Q, Texas and the other big chains have one price, builders' merchants have always had a *trade price* for their builder customers and a *retail price* for consumers. With the competition as it is you will find that in many merchants now the gap between trade and retail narrows considerably according to the size and worth of your purchase.

In many respects, the builders' merchant is a better bet for getting what you want because he will carry a larger variety of stock (to satisfy the trade) and at the same time he employs qualified trade staff who are more experienced in dealing with building products and can therefore offer good advice on their applications.

The Builders' Merchants Federation is now very keen to encourage homeowners to use their members and is putting more effort into marketing their services to the public. Many merchants have now developed larger showrooms, complete with room settings to give householders ideas for their kitchen, bathroom and other refurbishing schemes. It is certainly worth contacting the Federation for details of their member services. See the Addresses section at the back of this book – for this and other sources of information which could be helpful to you in planning and starting your project.

SORTING OUT THE BASICS

At the very least your house must be proof against the elements and intruders. But it is energy efficient. Are the domestic services installed properly and working safely? Only when you have attended to the basics do all the other improvements and embellishments become worthwhile.

First and foremost, a house has to be proof against the elements and intruders. It has to be energy efficient and have the essential domestic services. It is only when these vital aspects of your home have been attended to that other improvements and embellishments become worthwhile.

There is, after all, little point in creating a sumptuous bedroom if you have to have a bucket in the corner to catch the drips from a leaking roof. How can you enjoy being the gourmet cook with all the latest equipment and gadgetry if, when you use them, the whole house might catch fire through faulty electrical wiring? And you can hardly relax in your redesigned living room if the floor is being eaten up by woodworm, while the damp is rising up the wall to the draughty, insecure window which burglars can enter .

THE TOP PRIORITY

Roofs are high up and awkward to get at safely, so they are not often looked at very closely. Deterioration is therefore usually spotted at rather a late stage. By the time the first worn-out tile or slate has come crashing down into your garden, there are probably a fair number on the verge of doing the same – but when? And with what effect?

Patching is perhaps the most tempting way to repair a faulty roof because it does not take very long, nor does it cost much to do it. In fact, if you have an otherwise perfectly good roof, but tiles have been broken by, say, a television aerial falling down in a gale, it is the obvious and sensible solution. But if other parts of the roof require attention the probability is that the whole roof is on the way to failure.

Top priorities:

1 Crumbling chimney stacks and loose chimney pots are dangerous and should be rebedded and repointed.

2 Ridges normally need attention more often than the rest of the roof. If the ridge is in a poor state, the whole roof should be thoroughly checked.

3 Damaged, loose or missing slates or tiles let in rain which can cause costly damage to roof timbers and to other parts of the structure as well as ruining decoration. Falling slates are very dangerous.

4 Flashing where the roof joins an abutment or chimney may be of zinc, which can fail through corrosion or leakage at mortar joints. Defective flashings should be replaced with lead when you re-roof.

5 Cement or tile fillets are cheaper than lead flashing and are often used at abutments. But cracks can be caused by movement and frost action can lead to water penetration.

6 Copings can come loose and when deterioration is evident these should be rebedded and repointed.

7 Valleys can be the first parts of a roof to leak. Valley welts and linings can fail and movement can create cracks and holes which are difficult to repair.

8 Blocked gutters impede the flow of water from the roof.

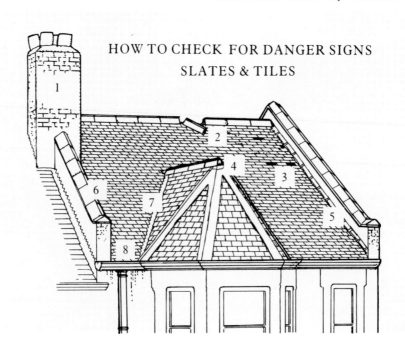

HOW TO CHECK FOR DANGER SIGNS
SLATES & TILES

Another option for treating a failing roof is to use one of the protective coatings which can be applied over slates or tiles. Once it hardens, the coating seals the gaps and holds the tiles in place. The problem is, that many of these treatments crack when natural movement takes place and it then becomes very hard to find the source of subsequent leaks. Furthermore, sealing the roof restricts the circulation of air which is essential to prevent timber decay in roof spaces. While there is some acceptance of this process, it is not recommended according to British Standards.

It is fairly easy to see when a roof is starting to fail and while the illustration on the opposite page shows rather more faults than any one roof would normally have, it does highlight just about all the particular problems that can arise. Another important tell-tale sign of a roof on the way out is when the tiles start to spall – to flake – due to frost and weather. With slates, their fixing holes start wearing, which means that they will slide off the roof very easily. Slate roofs can also suffer from nail sickness – when the fixing nails rust away – leaving the covering in a very unstable condition.

While leaks and loose tiles are obvious symptoms of a problem with the roof, it may be that the covering is still in a decent enough condition, but that the actual structure on the inside has developed some major fault. Timbers can become weakened by infestation or damp or, as happened with the house featured in the '*Halifax House of Home Improvement*' video, the roof was trying to do 'the splits' – and so had to come off completely.

There is no doubt that reroofing is a job for the professionals. Under the Health and Safety Act of 1974 a scaffold should be used and this will be costed in by the contractor. All the existing roof coverings and battens have to be removed – with the timbers carefully checked for any signs of decay or structural failure – and then overlapping felt underlay is fitted and secured with new tiling battens. The tiles are then laid – and if modern interlocking single-lap tiles are used this will be both economical in battening and quick to lay. Everything should be done in accordance with British Standard 5534

(Slating and Tiling).

The roof, ridge and verge tiles are then secured either by bedding in cement mortar as on the hipped Halifax House or they can be secured with a Dry Fix System such as the one specially developed by Marley for gable roofs. This is obviously the moment to deal with any renewal of lead work and chimney flashings or the repointing of any brickwork, such as chimneys and parapet walls.

While natural slate and clay tiles are certainly available at a price the vast majority of reroofing in this country is now carried out with modern concrete tiles. These are produced in a variety of different profiles, granular and smooth faces and such is the technology that the products can be guaranteed for the life expectancy of the property. What cannot be so readily guaranteed is the contractor's workmanship. It makes sense, therefore, to seek advice about local roofing contractors from the National Federation of Roofing contractors, or deal with an Allied Roofing Merchant – from the national association of local roofing materials suppliers.

Modern concrete tiles will last a lifetime, and it makes sense to ensure that the dressing for valleys and the flashing of chimneys will last equally long. Lead is the best material to use.

Hidden chamber: today's drainage
systems do not depend on the
old-fashioned brick-built
inspection chambers for access;
this simple, preformed type
involves a fraction of the labour
that used to be needed.

A drainage pipeline being
connected to an existing sewer.
The local authority have the right
to, and will, inspect and test your
work under the Building
Regulations.

A hopper with back inlet for
making an indirect connection of
waste or rainwater entries.

A layout of vitrified clay pipes with
mechanical push-fit joints will
require no maintenance once
properly installed. Note the
rodding point at the head of the
drain to clear any blockage.

DRAINAGE

It is reckoned that something over
three-quarters of a million gallons of
rainwater will fall on your roof during its
lifetime – and it all has to go somewhere.
Indeed, the 4,000 litres of waste water
and sewerage produced by the average
householed *each day* also needs to be
disposed of efficiently. Yet drainage is
one of those things we all expect to be
working properly, so it is a topic very
much out of sight and out of mind – until
something goes wrong.

There are two separate types of
drainage. One set of drains normally
conducts all the 'surface water'
splashing down on your roof, lawn and
drive to a constructed soakaway in the
ground or else to a pond, natural stream
or other suitable discharge point. The
'foul water' – sewerage, bath water and
washing-up water – flows into the main
drainage system which runs outside
your house.

The guttering system from your roof
together with any storm drains which
you might have outside a garage or in a

yard will normally be channelled to a
soakaway, so that the water can slowly
disperse into the ground. It is always
advisable to have a rodding point
incorporated so that if the drain does get
blocked by any debris, it can easily be
cleared with a set of rodding equipment
(*see illustration*). So far as the foul water
is concerned, this is normally piped
straight into the main sewerage system
which usually runs across either the
back or the front of your house.
However, there are still many propertjes
in the country which are not on a main
drainage system and the house (or
sometimes a whole estate) has to rely on
a septic tank or cesspool.

While a cesspool is simply a storage
tank for all the raw sewerage and has to
be emptied regularly (it is, not
surprisingly, illegal to allow a cesspool
to overflow), a septic tank is a
sewerage-treatment system which,
depending on its size and use, will only
have to be de-sludged by the local
authority once or twice a year. A
properly sited, well-constructed and
efficient septic tank is almost as good as

CESSPOOL

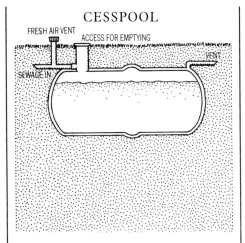

FRESH AIR VENT — ACCESS FOR EMPTYING

VENT

SEWAGE IN

being on main drainage. All it requires is a few centimetres of operating head to maintain a flow through the tank; it is non-mechanical, consumes no power, is noiseless and can survive for long periods of inactivity with no impairment to its operational effectiveness.

ALBION SOAKAWAY

EFFLUENT IN

EFFLUENT SOAKS OUT INTO LOWER STRATA OF SOIL

SUB-SURFACE IRRIGATION FROM A SEPTIC TANK

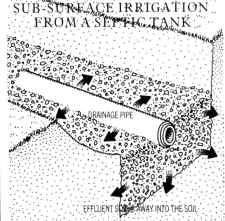

DRAINAGE PIPE

EFFLUENT SOAKS AWAY INTO THE SOIL

Septic tanks work on a very simple principle. They provide quiescent conditions to enable all the coarse,

suspended solids to settle out; the accumulated sludge is digested by an anaerobic bacteria to break down the solids. Following this primary stage of purification, the best method of disposal of the effluent is through sub-surface irrigation – but it is dependent on the porosity of the topsoil and the gradient of the ground, because the effluent must flow away without backing up, particularly in wet winter conditions.

Unlike the Halifax House which had to have its total drainage system renewed, it is more probable that you will only be adding to an existing system because of putting in, say, a second

SEPTIC TANK

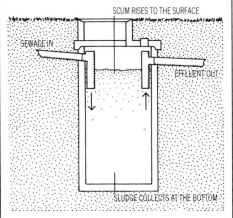

SCUM RISES TO THE SURFACE

SEWAGE IN

EFFLUENT OUT

SLUDGE COLLECTS AT THE BOTTOM

bathroom or as a result of refurbishing a kitchen. Obviously, you will need to have the existing system checked out by a surveyor and have the extension to it designed by him. However, the actual laying of a new drainage pipe is a simple enough DIY job – made somewhat easier by using an excavator to cut the actual trench.

Despite the advent of plastic pipes – which are now normally used for gutters and downpipes – there is no doubt that vitrified clay is still the proven, durable system to use. The plain-end pipes and fittings of the Hepworth SuperSleve system, for example, together with their mechanical push-fit joints, make the whole operation very straightforward.

The pipeline must be laid with an even fall so that it will flow smoothly and you will need to provide access at the head of each drain run, at a change of direction and at or near pipe junctions. At key positions along the run of pipes, you will need to install access units and you can now get ready-made inspection

A cess pool is simply a storage tank for all raw sewage; it has to be emptied regularly.

A septic tank is a sewage-treatment system; it needs de-sludging once or twice a year.

Following the primary stage of purification, if the ground is very porous, effluent can be introduced to the lower strata of soil by means of a concrete soakaway.

The effluent from a septic tank is usually disposed of by sub-surface irrigation – soaking away from pipes into the soil.

When the trench is filled in, the polypropylene inspection chamber – capped with a cast iron lid – gives convenient access in the unlikely event of a blockage.

For drains at the shallow depths usual for most domestic systems, vitrified clay inspection chambers can be used.

Pipework should be tested before the trench is back-filled by carefully compacting selected material from the excavation, by hand. Distribute the material equally on both sides of the pipes to buttress them against the side of the trench. Once 300 mm of this material has been filled in above the crown of the pipes, the remainder of the excavated material can be compacted mechanically.

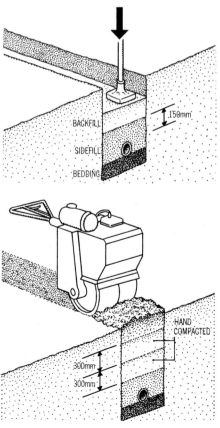

chambers to eliminate the toil and trouble of building old-fashioned brick ones. Naturally, the whole system has to be watertight and the local authority will have to supervise a mandatory test before the trench is back-filled (in layers to allow for settlement) and the ground reinstated.

A house simply can't exist without a good drainage system and, while you will need professional help with the design, the actual task of laying the pipes has been made very simple through modern technology.

DAMPNESS AND TIMBER DECAY

With a sound roof and a good drainage system, the water which pours on to your property should be safely channelled into the ground without impairing the structure of your house. However, water may still rise up through the walls or penetrate the brickwork.

Older buildings which do not have cavity walls are much more prone to water penetration through the brickwork, and in very badly affected cases complete repointing may be necessary. Otherwise, an exterior water-proofer sprayed on the surface of the walls will create a water-repellent barrier. Such products are usually based on either silicone or titanium and will not affect the appearance of the surface after application, although it is always advisable to treat a small test area first.

RISING DAMP

Rising damp is the most common cause of wetness in walls and, if left long enough, it can have a serious affect on timber floors and supporting joists in contact with the damp wall. The source of the dampness needs to be investigated carefully as the true cause of the problem may well turn out to be something like a broken downpipe or a flowerbed with too much earth piled up against the wall, forming a 'bridge' over a perfectly good damp course.

The most common solution for a defective or non-existent damp proof course is to inject a chemical into the wall, which cures on drying to form a permanent and continuous waterproof barrier. The chemical used should conform to BS 3826, and is injected at the base of the exterior walls at a depth

and level depending on each application. The problem with rising damp is that it not only damages the plaster on the inside of the wall but brings with it various salts from the soil which get deposited as the water evaporates. If the damaged plaster is simply removed and replaced with conventional plaster, the chances are that the salts left in the wall will attract water vapour from the air in the room and this will damage the new plaster and cause stains on the decorations. It is essential, therefore, that specially formulated water-repellent plaster is used, to a height of not less than 3 feet above the floor, as part of the overall damp-proofing treatment.

WET AND DRY ROT

Dampness in buildings can cause fungal spores to germinate and feed on wood, resulting in decay which, if left untreated for long periods, can cause structural failure. There are two types of wood rot and each one requires a completely different method of treatment.

Wet rot

Wet rot occurs when timber is subjected to constant damp conditions – like rain constantly soaking a poorly maintained window frame or floor joists which have been continually soaked by, say, a broken downpipe beneath the ground. As soon as the source of damp is removed the wet rot will stop and the timber can be dealt with.

Dry rot

Dry rot is a very different story. It is a fungus with a strong and distinctive smell that spreads very rapidly. It has the ability to store up reserves of food so that it can continue to grow long after the source of moisture has dried up. Affected timber must be cut out and burnt and any wood up to a metre away must also be removed. All brickwork and plaster close to the attack must be treated with a proprietary fungicide and a wood preservative should be applied to all existing and replacement timber. Total eradication is absolutely vital.

TIMBER INFESTATION

Timber can be attacked by a number of different wood-boring insects such as the common furniture beetle, death

watch beetle, the powder post beetle and the house long horn beetle. Each can cause a varying amount of damage and at the slightest sign the appropriate insecticide must be injected under pressure into the woodworm holes and all accessible surfaces treated. In the case of a bad attack timbers may have to be replaced.

Woodworm attack is mainly found in the roof timbers of attics, but once in the

The most common solution to a defective damp proof course is to inject a chemical (conforming to BS 3826) into the wall – this forms a continuous and long-lasting waterproof barrier.

Woodworm-infested floor boards have to be removed, and the remaining boards treated to prevent the infestation spreading.

Wet rot occurs when timber is constantly subjected to damp conditions. Ground floors are commonly affected in this way, often by leakage from broken downpipes.

house all floor joists, floorboards and, of course, furniture becomes vulnerable and thorough treatment is required. Some 75 per cent of the woodworm damage in the UK is done by the common furniture beetle and, while there are plenty of DIY kits available, if structural timbers are infested it is best to get professional treatment.

Dampness and timber decay in buildings cannot be taken lightly and the remedial treatment needs to be carried out thoroughly – with the work guaranteed, so that, when the time comes, a prospective purchaser will not have any qualms about the property. So which companies should you use? One firm, Rentokil, dominates the market. Bearing in mind that this is an industry where some 600 new companies start up each year and about the same number go out of business, a small firm's guarantee can by no means always be counted on!

Woodworm attack is mainly found in roof timbers, and it is best to call in a professional firm to treat the infected area.

In an effort to combat this problem, the Guaranteed Treatments Protection Trust (GTPT) was formed in 1983 and is open to all members of the British Wood Preserving Association (BWPA) and the British Chemical Dampcourse Association (BCDA). Under the scheme the GTPT holds a master insurance policy so that if a contractor is not available to meet a claim, the GTPT will stand in place of that contractor and honour the guarantee. It is a good idea that needs encouraging, but as with all insurance policies, much depends on its renewal year by year.

At the moment only about 10 per cent of the total number of firms in the market belong to either the BWPA or BCDA and less than half of those have joined the GTPT, so it remains an uphill struggle for the scheme to become firmly established.

Rentokil has already been in business for 50 years and has so far not joined the scheme – preferring to stand on its own reputation and company guarantee. Incidentally, the company also has an insurance policy to protect any part of your house which did not require treatment but might still be open to attack at a later date. This is because there is simply no effective barrier against the beetle deciding to fly into your house again and taking up residence.

WATER AND ELECTRICS

There can be very few houses in this country which have neither water nor electricity laid on – although in 1979 I had to get both services down half a mile of lane to a game-keeper's cottage, which is now my home, and a very traumatic and expensive business it was! These days we expect to turn a tap or flick a switch to get an instant response. In fact, it is really only when things go wrong that we are conscious of either service and what is entailed in keeping them working properly.

Water

Water arrives at your property, under pressure, as part of the water authority's mains system and terminates at a stopcock at your boundary. From then on, it is your responsibility. In case of emergency, you should know exactly where the water authority's stopcock is located, although it can usually only be turned by one of the authority's turnkeys.

The service pipe then enters your property at a depth of about 3 feet, usually in or near the kitchen where you will find the main stopcock. You should make sure that everyone in your household knows where it is, in case of emergency. From there, the mains will rise (hence the term 'rising main') to probably not more than four connections. The first will be to the cold tap over the kitchen sink for drinking water and cooking purposes. If you have an outside tap for a garage or garden the connection will be close to the branch for the kitchen sink – and it is important to have a further stopcock at this point so that, in winter, you can drain down the

The electronic revolution has meant an enormous growth in the number of electric appliances in our homes. Ten years ago, for example, there were no videos and no microwaves; today, these are used in 5 million and 3 million homes respectively.

outside tap as a precaution against frost damage.

The rising main will then go on up to your loft where it will feed the cold water storage tank, as well as the expansion tank if you have an indirect hot water system. It could also feed an instantaneous electric shower, if you need it. Otherwise, all the other cold water services are supplied by pipes taken from the cold water storage system – to basins, baths and for the hot water storage cylinder.

It is only sensible that each distribution pipe should be able to be isolated without affecting the rest of the household water supply, so that you can renew taps and washers. This is done by fitting gate valves. Incidentally, it is a good tip to turn all your stopcocks and gate valves on and off a couple of times a year to ensure that they have not become jammed in position. There can be nothing worse than one that sticks on you when you most need to use it – in an emergency! Furthermore, they need to be checked periodically to see that they are not weeping or dripping in any way. (There is nothing that dry rot likes better than a gently dripping stopcock on to a wooden floor in a gloomy corner of an airless cupboard under the sink!)

Before you carry out any improvements, it is obviously essential to know the general geography of your plumbing. If you are going to convert your loft you will inevitably have to move the water tanks and pipes around. If you are adding a second bathroom you will need to extend the services and if

you are thinking of revamping your kitchen or simply installing a washing machine, the plumbing is going to be involved. However, the main plumbing application these days is all tied in with the central heating of the house and this will be dealt with in chapter six.

Electrics

Electricity arrives at your house in much the same way as the water; it terminates at the meter and from that point it is your responsibility to ensure its safe distribution and use around the house. However, even more so than water, it is an instant menace when something goes wrong. So your whole electrical system needs to be treated with the utmost respect.

Every year 50 people are killed in electrical accidents in the home and over 4,900 fires are started through faulty electrics. Many of these tragedies could have been avoided.

If you are buying a house to do up, one of your very first steps should be to have an electrical survey, for if the house has not been re-wired in the last 25 to 30 years, it could well be a most hazardous place. Electrical components manufacturer, MK Electric, has organised a free electrical survey service and if you write to the company it will put you in touch with an independent, properly qualified electrical contractor to inspect your complete wiring system and advise you on what should be done, according to the needs of the house and your personal requirements.

Houses built before the early 1950s

had electrical circuits of rubber-covered cable and were designed to accommodate products with round pin plugs. The problem with rubber is that it deteriorates with age, becoming brittle and eventually falling away from the copper current-carrying conductors – thus leaving them exposed and creating a dangerous fire risk. The wiring supporting the sockets was installed in what is known as a radial system, whereby each socket was fed by its own cable from the main consumer unit.

The modern wiring system uses what is known as a ring circuit and this means that the cable leaves the fuse in the fuse box, goes round in a loop and returns back to the fuse. Up to 10 socket outlets may be tapped in at intervals and all of these are of a common size and dimension to allow for plugs with a flat pin. Within each plug is a fuse for electrical protection and this fuse should always match the rating of the domestic appliance for which it is being used.

In any old house the wiring may not only be in a poor condition but it is also likely that there is a totally insufficient number of power points to cater for modern demands on electricity. Back in 1959, the Building Research Station produced a report which concluded that in a house designed for five people about 15 electrical points were required to meet the 'reasonable present day needs'; if you consider the dramatic growth in the use of electrical equipment and appliances from that time to the present day, you will appreciate just how many more power points are really necessary nowadays. In fact, in 1986 the Electrical Installation Industry Liaison Committee (EIILC) produced a report which recommended the following minimum requirements for an average house:

ROOM	MINIMUM
Kitchen	4
Living Room	6
Dining Room	3
Double bedroom	4
Single bedroom/study	3
Single bed-sitting room	4
Landing/stairs	1
Hall	1
Garage	2
Store/workroom	1
Central heating boiler point	1

a. Each outlet to be of the twin switch type.
b. The central heating boiler socket facility is shown as a separate item as its location can vary according to the dwelling.
c. A separate individual circuit should be provided for each immersion heater incorporating a double pole switch of appropriate rating.

Towards the end of the 1950s the nation was spending £400 million a year on all types of electric and electronic household goods. This has now increased to an annual £5,000 million.

This enormous increase in electrical gadgetry around the house makes safety an even more important matter. Whether your house needs rewiring or not it may well be sensible to replace your old fuse box with a modern consumer unit. While the old-style fuses are perfectly safe in themselves, when one blows it always seems to be on an occasion when you have run out of the correct-gauge fuse wire. This leads to the temptation to use anything from a paper clip to a bent nail to get the system working again. The result could mean an undetected overload – and a fire.

Much safer and less fiddly to install is a miniature circuit breaker (MCB) which is a permanently sealed unit pre-set by the manufacturer, so that all you have to do to restore electrical power is to throw back a switch. It is much more convenient, and abuse-proof.

The unit can also have built into it what is called an earth leakage circuit breaker (ELCB). This device constantly monitors the flow of electricity around your house so that whenever it detects a short circuit anywhere it immediately earths the current. This way it will turn what could have been a fatal shock into a

Earth Leakage Circuit Breaker constantly monitors the flow of electricity around your house. Whenever it detects a short circuit it immediately earths the current to prevent what could be a fatal shock.

small jolt. Such protection is particularly relevant when using mains equipment out of doors, such as electrically operated lawnmowers, hedge trimmers and other power tools.

The latest wiring regulations recommend the use of ELCBs in workshops, garages and other such situations. It is an inexpensive operation to replace an existing double socket with a product such as the Sentry socket, which incorporates an ELCB.

When it comes to employing an electrician, always make sure he is a fully qualified, registered contractor who is on the approved roll of the National Inspection Council for Electrical Installation Contracting (NICEIC). There are more than 8,000 contractors registered throughout the country and the NICEIC has inspecting engineers who make regular visits to ensure that their work complies with the wiring regulations.

Many contractors (provided they are on the roll of the NICEIC) belong to the Electrical Contractors Association which runs a guarantee scheme to cover member firms' workmanship and contractual obligations.

ENERGY EFFICIENCY

Ever since the world fuel crisis in the mid 1970s we have had to pay dearly for our energy. Fuel bills – for electricity, gas, oil or solid fuel – now form a major part of any family's budget. It is therefore vital that any home is as energy efficient as possible.

Up to 80 per cent of the fuel we buy is spent on providing heating and hot water and in chapter 6 the pros and cons

of the different systems and methods available are considered. But whatever you choose, you have to face the fact that all the heat produced in a home is eventually lost to the atmosphere and that the quicker it is lost the more expensive it becomes. The prime object must be to slow down the rate of heat loss as much as possible from the fabric of the building and to do this in the most cost effective way.

While there are several precise calculations which can be made to establish the heat loss through the different materials that are used in the construction of a house, you will not be far out if you consider that up to a third of your heat loss will be through the roof, a third through the walls and the balance through the windows, doors and floors.

THE ROOF

The considerable publicity in recent years for loft insulation, combined with the grant available under the Homes Insulation Scheme, must mean that most roofs in this country are now insulated. But it is certainly worth checking whether yours has been done to the old standard of 1 inch (30mm) or to the currently recommended thickness of 4 inches (100mm). It is also vital that your cold water tank and all the pipes are properly lagged for frost protection. For the average house the cost of the materials for loft insulation should be no more than the saving you will make in just 1 year on your fuel bill, so it is obviously a most cost-effective improvement and should be done as a matter of priority.

It is inexpensive to replace an existing double socket with a Sentry socket, which incorporates an earth leakage circuit breaker. This could be a life-saver when using electric equipment outdoors.

First step in loft insulation: Clear away any debris between the joists, and sweep up the dust – it is important that the surface should be clean before you lay any insulation material.

2 Place a sturdy board across the joists for standing or kneeling safely while laying the material. Always start at the eaves, ensuring you leave a gap for ventilation, and unroll towards the centre of the loft.

3 Cut and butt ends together so all the surface is covered, but do not insulate under water tanks.

4 If possible, lay insulation under pipes and wires, but take care not to damage. Push the material into the eaves, but not so far that it blocks the air gap.

5 Don't forget to insulate top of the loft trapdoor. Ensure that the trap fits properly and is draughtproof.

6 If the roof is boarded or felted under the tiles, it is essential to leave a gap at the eaves to allow ventilation to the roof space. Seal any cracks around pipes and cables where they pass through the ceiling.

7 When using a granular insulating material, use a strip of wood to level across the joists.

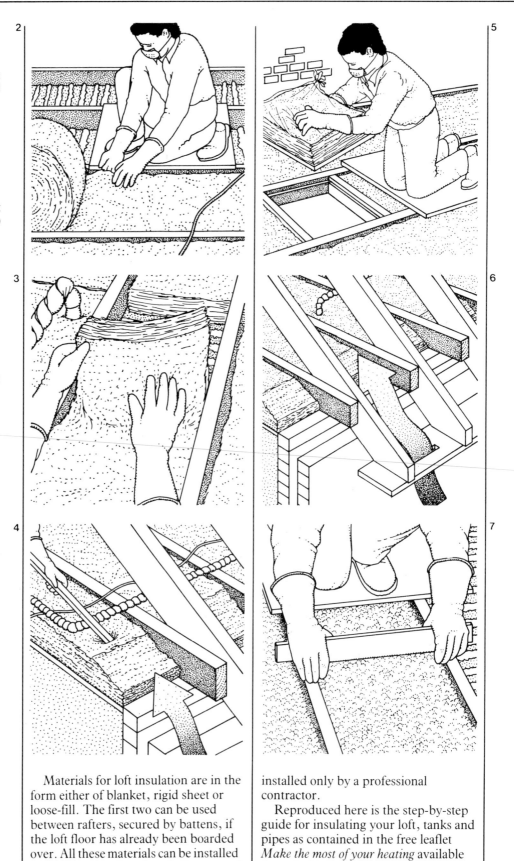

Materials for loft insulation are in the form either of blanket, rigid sheet or loose-fill. The first two can be used between rafters, secured by battens, if the loft floor has already been boarded over. All these materials can be installed as a DIY project (see above). One type of material, blown-in fibre, which is hosed into the loft by air pressure, should be installed only by a professional contractor.

Reproduced here is the step-by-step guide for insulating your loft, tanks and pipes as contained in the free leaflet *Make the most of your heating* available from the Energy Efficiency Office, Room 1312, Thames House South, Millbank, London SW1P 4QJ.

THE WALLS

If your house was built with cavity walls, filling the gap between the inner and outer sections of the wall with an appropriate insulation material could cut your heat loss through the walls by half. It is not a DIY job and the work will need to be carried out under the terms of a current British Board of Agrement Certificate by an approved installation company. Probably the most common and certainly the least expensive product to use is urea formaldehyde (UF) foam provided this is installed in accordance with the relevant requirements. The formaldehyde given off as the UF foam cures can cause a certain amount of discomfort and irritation, so it must be installed correctly and in the right circumstances. The British Standards Institution has established a surveillance scheme under which firms conducting installation can register, and it is advisable to use such a firm.

The other approved methods of filling the cavity include the use of expanded polystyrene beads and granules which are blown, by low air pressure, into the cavity. There is also a similar product, which is coated with an adhesive while it is being blown into the cavity; this dries quickly to make the beads stick together to form a stable, low-porous mass within the cavity wall.

Another method of cavity fill is to blow spun rock or glass fibres, which have been treated to make them water repellent, into the holes drilled through the outer leaf. This method – as with all the others – is subject to a Certificate and there is a hot line for checking on or obtaining a list of approved firms at the Board – 0923 662900.

There is no doubt that cavity wall insulation is a sound investment. Depending on the type and size of your house, it will show a payback period of between four and seven years at current fuel prices. the price only has to go up, yet again, after the work has been completed and your payback period will be even shorter. However, if your house is unsuitable for cavity insulation there are ways of beefing up a solid wall, either from the inside or the outside. But this is a more costly and disruptive method with the price for an average house starting at about £1500.

The internal method of solid wall insulation is very similar to that of constructing a 'stud' wall with plasterboard (this is described in chapter 11). The clear advantage over any external operation is that you can do it room by room and it has no effect on the general appearance of the house – but you do lose an inch or two of space.

Insulation can of course be applied to the outside walls above the damp proof course level. This usually involves covering the whole area with a protective coat of rendering or else the insulating material is, itself, made as part of a thick coat of rendering. If your external walls are in poor condition anyway, this method is certainly worth considering but it will probably cost you thousands, rather than hundreds, of pounds.

WINDOWS, DOORS AND FLOORS

As the thinnest part of your house's skin, single-glazed windows lose up to a quarter of the heat you generate. While some of the heat is clearly lost through the panes, the greater loss is very often due to the cold draughts getting in, and the warm air escaping from, ill-fitting frames.

There are two ways of attacking the problem. One is to fit 'secondary' glazing, which is where you leave the existing window in place and add a second layer on the inside. The other, which applies when the windows are in poor condition and need replacing, is to install a new frame which incorporates a sealed unit of two sheets of glass – namely, double glazing.

With secondary glazing there are several very cheap methods of installation. You can attach flexible or rigid plastic sheets to the inside of the

Secondary glazing is the installing of an additional, separate inner window. It is the method of double glazing that best suits older houses which would not be suited to the modern style of double-glazed replacement windows.

Double glazed windows in hardwood frames look good as well as making a great deal of difference to the comfort of the room inside.

Old, perished frames should be replaced with new, hardwood ones before fitting new windows.

Aluminium double glazing can transfer the cold from outside through the metal frame. Here, a 'thermal break' separates the outer and inner metal parts of the frame and prevents the cold being conducted through.

frames which more or less put the windows out of commission – and might be dangerous in the case of a fire. Alternatively, you can fit a frame of rigid plastic or glass across each section so they can slide across the window sill to allow the window to be opend (and cleaned). There are plenty of DIY kits which you can use, provided you can measure and fit the system accurately. Good, professionally installed, secondary glazing will certainly make a great deal of difference to the comfort of the room. It should significantly reduce condensation and cut down external noise, too.

If, however, the original frames are in poor condition – like the old metal frames on the mid-1930s house featured in the Halifax home improvement video project (*see photograph*) – new sealed unit double glazing will make a world of difference. These units are not cheap, so if you are going to double-glaze all or part of your house, it is sensible to investigate and evaluate the technical features offered by the various manufacturers. For the Halifax house,

the double-glazed units were manufactured by Therm-A-Stor and there are two particular points about their manufacturing process which are specifically worth noting:

Thermal break

The inner frames of the windows are completely insulated from the outside by a thermal break – with the cavity insulated with close cell polyurethane foam. From the picture you will see what a dramatic affect there is, when compared with a standard type of window frame.

Thermagas

The 20mm space between the sealed units of the glass is filled with a special formulation of inert gases. These have several times the density of air and when fed into the sealed glazing unit they act as a transparent thermal blanket. The gases also give stronger acoustic insulation, noticeably boosting sound proofing.

Professionally installed double glazing cannot justify its cost on energy efficiency grounds alone. In most cases, the payback period would be a considerable time and it should be regarded as an investment in the property. Since we live in a very noisy age, it is by the same token that many houses need double glazing to allow the occupants to live in peace and quiet

within the turmoil of large cities – and in traffic-choked towns and villages. The comfort of a draught-free and relatively quiet home, of course, thoroughly justifies an investment in good double glazing.

BEATING THE DRAUGHTS

All windows (which are not being double glazed) and doors can be draught-proofed by using any one of a number of different types of seals. A quick, cheap way of dealing with the problem is to use self-adhesive foam strips which can be bought in rolls at any hardware store. However, they become grubby with use and will not last very long. A better, more durable method is to use nylon, polypropylene, rubber or what is known as plastic atomic strip.

A more recent innovation is the wiper seal which incorporates a fine nylon brush, which is particularly good for sash windows and sliding doors. One method especially well suited to casement windows and conventional swinging doors is to use a silicone rubber sealant to form a permanently flexible, in-situ, gasket.

You can buy a kit comprising two cartridges of Dow Corning 781 Silicone Sealant, skeleton gun, primer, low tack tape and cleaner (they can also all be bought separately) to produce a tight seal that won't crack and will provide a maintenance-free seal for a service life in excess of 30 years. The step-by-step illustrated guide (*opposite*) shows you exactly what to do and it really is a simple DIY job.

Floors are another place where draughts enter and heat departs. While it is quite a performance, you can take the floorboards up and drape netting over all the joists in order to lay mineral-fibre mat as a means of insulation – taking care not to block the underfloor ventilation which protects the joists from dampness and rot. Alternatively, you can use a sealant between the gaps in the floorboards and at the skirting, and make sure that you use a good felt or rubber underlay beneath your carpet.

The nation's annual energy bill stands at some £35,000 million, about half of which is accounted for in buildings. It is reckoned that more than £3,000 million of that cost could be saved per year.

With such huge figures at stake, the Department of the Environment has published a guide to *Energy Efficient Renovation of Houses* and the Energy Efficiency Office has collaborated with the Consumers' Association to produce a parallel guide, *Energy Savings with Home Improvement*. Both the building industry and householders seeking further information can find invaluable advice on energy efficiency from these publications.

1 Ill-fitting windows let in draughts and waste heat. A made-to-measure silicone rubber gasket can be formed round the frame, compresses when the window is shut, and makes for a really well-sealed fit.

2 All surfaces must be clean, dry and free from loose aggregate, oils, grease etc. Any flaky paint should be removed down to the wood. A special primer has to be applied, and this should be dry in about half an hour.

3 On the mating surface, where the gasket is not to adhere (usually the opening frame), apply a low-tack tape. Alternatively, vaseline or mineral jelly is suitable – but be careful not to get it on the surfaces where the gasket will be bonded.

4 Gun on sufficient sealant to form an adequate seal when compressed, all the way round the opening. Initially, there is a vinegary smell of acetic acid, but this will disappear in a few hours as the sealant cures.

5 Close the window gently to press the sealant into shape and secure it with the catch in the lightly closed position.

6 The surplus sealant squeezed out can be neatly removed with a knife or spatula, but the window must not be opened for at least 48 hours to ensure that the gasket has properly cured.

7 When first opening the window, prise it at one corner so undue force is not needed. (Note that the sealant is available in a range of colours as well as the grey in the pictures.)

8 Excess sealant may be cleaned off tools and non-porous surfaces with a silicon cleaner before it cures. Sealant adhering to porous surfaces should be left until just cured, then removed by abrasion.

HOME SECURITY

With a burglary now taking place every minute of every day and night, it is imperative that your home becomes, within reason, a veritable fortress against intruders. Security must today be regarded as one of the basic improvements to carry out as a matter of priority.

Before you do *anything*, contact your local Police Station and ask if a Crime Prevention Officer (CPO) can call at your house to advise you on the best means of securing your property. CPOs are specially trained, full-time serving police officers who advise the public in the security field. You will find that the CPO will offer cost-effective, value-for-money recommendations and it is very worth while getting this free, unbiased survey before you contact any security firms.

Since 90 per cent of burglaries are carried out by opportunists looking for easy pickings, your priority should be *physical security* to stop intruders getting in. If you simply make your doors and windows secure you will do much to deter the vast majority of burglars. If a thief can't get in – or at least it is very difficult for him to do so – your property is very much less at risk.

Doors
A lock is only as strong as the door and frame to which it is fitted, so it is important to check these first. It's all very well having a good-looking door, but if it is largely glass or thin panels an

SORTING OUT THE BASICS

intruder can remove the wood work surrounding the lock in a number of ways – brute force often being the simplest. He can then put his hand round to open the door by turning the knob of an ordinary night-latch and by pulling back any surface-mounted bolts. In those circumstances the thief not only gains entry but has an easy exit – from which he can take quite large items such as a television set.

Doors should be fitted with either a surface-mounted dead latch, that is, one that can be locked solid in the extended position, or fitted with a mortice lock in the outside closing edge of the door itself. As an extra precaution a dead latch or rim lock can – by a 'double-locking' mechanism – be deadlocked when the key is turned in both directions (from the outside). This way both the bolt and the inside knob are deadlocked simultaneously.

Patio doors supplied by leading manufacturers will usually have toughened double glazing and patio

door locks, factory-fitted and designed to prevent any form of forced entry. Let the CPO advise on the suitability of the ones fitted to yours; patio doors can be excellent 'final exits' and it is important that yours isn't!

It is vital that all the doors in your house can be deadlocked, so that if a burglar gets in through a window he will not be able to get out through the doors. This makes it much more risky for him and will mean that he cannot take large items out. The CPO, when he visits you, will tell you about using concealed mortice bolts, door chains or limiters, door viewers and other security devices.

Another important security aspect of external doors is that of lighting. An outside light that illuminates your front door makes anyone on your doorstep that much more visible, both to passers by and to you when you open the door. Such a light is certainly a good idea anyway, for illuminating the way for you or your visitors – invited ones, that is – to see the way to your door.

DEADLATCH

Where a door is too thin to contain a mortice lock, a surface-mounted rim lock should be fitted. With a 'double-locking' mechanism when the key is turned in both directions from the outside, the bolt and the inside knob are deadlocked simultaneously.

A two-lever lock has only 24 keys before a repeat, whereas a five-lever one has 1,000. The difference in price is well worth the improvement in security.

MORTICE LOCKS

Made for fitting into the outside closing edge of the door, a mortice lock should only used where the thickness of the wood is two inches or more. In a thinner door, the lock would weaken the structure, defeating its own object!

Although two-thirds of all break-ins are through insecure windows, burglars look for an escape route which is very often the back door. So fit a secure lock, and always remove the key when you go out. Hide the key in a safe place.

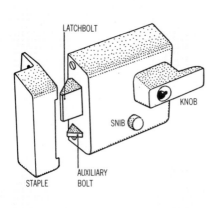

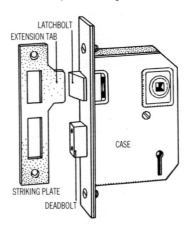

Windows

The majority of break-ins are through windows – especially those at the back of a property and on the ground floor. Glass, unless it is laminated or toughened, breaks very easily and if the window is unlocked it makes a simple access for the burglar.

It really is important that you fit locks to all the windows on the ground floor and, also, those upstairs which can be easily reached via a drainpipe, flat roof or other structure. There are any number of casement, sash and fanlight locks available and you can also get window arm locks which will add to the thief's difficulties. You can also get special locks for louvre windows and because the glass slates can be easily taken out, it is important that you fix them in with a strong adhesive.

Fitting security devices to windows around the house is the sort of project which one always means to do, but never seems to get round to – until it's too late! So do make burglary prevention an early priority, being sure at least to secure your windows and doors.

Burglar alarms

There are a number of misconceptions about burglar alarm systems. One is that they cost a lot of money. Another is that while they are always going off, no one takes any notice of them. A third is that the box outside your house advertises that you have valuables to protect.

While some sophisticated systems certainly cost four figure sums, there are now many DIY alarm kits on the market priced at under £200. If an alarm system is used properly it will certainly discourage most burglars – who will not be keen to stay in premises where the police or a keyholder could turn up at any minute. Furthermore, the fact that an alarm bell is visible outside your home has been proven to deter burglars. Some insurance companies will even reduce their premiums if the bell box is clearly displayed at the front of the building.

A burglar alarm consists of three parts: a detection device, control panel and a warning system. The detection device can be a simple magnetic contact which if disturbed by opening a door or a window will trigger off the alarm if the control panel has been set. There are also vibration, sonic and ray detectors.

The control panels can vary in their degree of sophistication and the alarm systems can be either internal or external – perhaps sending an electronic message to a monitoring station which will telephone the police immediately. Perhaps the irritating part of any system is the necessary wiring of the installation and it is a concept which is best thought of *before* you have decided to repaint and decorate the inside of your house!

Safes

If you are having an extension built, this is a good time to consider putting in either a wall or floor safe. While both are excellent ideas in any case, there would be little or no additional cost for the installation of the safe while a wall is being built or a concrete floor being constructed.

A wall safe built into the back of a

Burglary points of entry. Statistics show where a burglar is most likely to try to break into your home – and where good security is therefore most likely to pay off.

BURGLARY – POINTS OF ENTRY

Somewhere, there is a burglary every minute of the day and night. Statistically, you have a 1 in 3 chance of being burgled during your lifetime.

Protect your home and discourage thieves by taking effective security measures **now**. Improved security starts here.

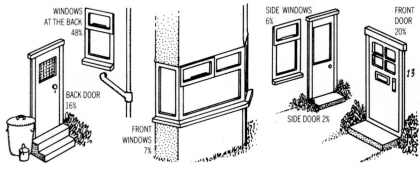

kitchen cupboard and screened from view by the contents will at least protect your jewellery and other small valuables, while giving you immediate access at the turn of a key. A floor safe hidden under a carpet would be very difficult for the quick in-and-out thief to find.

If you keep your passport in your safe at least it will jog your memory to lock away your valuables when you remove it to go on holiday abroad. It is also possible to get a small portable electronic safe to hide away your jewellery. When armed, the slightest movement will sound the alarm.

For valuables which you cannot put in a safe, like a glass cabinet containing a valuable collection of *objets d'art*, or a complete hi-fi system which is in constant use, there are two quite inexpensive products to help you secure them: the Fly and the Spider. The former is a small alarm box with a highly sensitive sensor which sounds an alarm at the slightest movement, while the other has four 'tentacles' which attach by sticky pads to protect a cluster of up to five valuable items. When switched on, any attempt to remove any of the protected items or to cut one of the tentacles sounds the alarm.

Lighting and marking

Not unnaturally, shady characters don't like being in the limelight! As well as keeping your front porch well lit at night you should also have good lighting at the back of your house. It is also a good idea to ensure that you have one or two time switches incorporated into your wiring so that the lights of different rooms can come on during the hours of darkness, when you are away from home.

Finally, for the price of about £1 you can buy a security marker pen to write your postcode followed by the number of your house or the first two letters of its name on all your valuables. While the fluid is visible until it dries it can only be seen under ultra violet light – which the police use to check all stolen or lost property. This way, if despite all you have done to improve your security a thief does get away with some of your property, there is a good chance of it finding its way back to you because it will be uniquely identified as belonging to you.

While it is possible that you might

inadvertently sit next to a burglar on a bus or a train, it is most unlikely that you are ever going to have a conversation with one – let alone find out all about the tricks of their abhorrent trade. But your local CPO will have 'met' quite a number in his time and know all about the techniques they employ, so he really is the person to survey your home and advise you on the best way of protecting it. So contact him – and, who knows, he may even show you or give you a leaflet about a home security video, made with Home Office support for the Halifax Home Improvement Video Library.

Identify your property. Mark your valuables with an ultra-violet marker pen with the postcode, followed by the house number. High-value items like jewellery should be photographed, and you should note a description, including details of hallmarks, identifying features, dents or blemishes.

Good security lighting provides a welcome to your invited guests.

YOUR GRAND DESIGN

Getting your home into the shape you want may mean remodelling some of the rooms. Your overall plan must take account of the fact that toddlers turn into teenagers, that old folks need special attention and that storage is a vital factor.

What makes a home? The people who live in it, quite obviously, but the environment of the home itself plays a large part, too.

When we first move house, the feelings emanating from it are those of the previous owners. It is almost as if we were camping out in their home. Even when our possessions are moved into position, it doesn't instantly 'feel right'.

It is best to make only the most simple changes straight away. Even live with a wallpaper you hate rather than rush to replace it – then regret your choice once you feel that you know the house better. Certainly resist the temptation to make sweeping changes in the kitchen layout when it would be very costly to get things wrong.

Live in your new home for a while before instigating any major alterations. This will give you a chance to decide more constructively what, if anything, really needs to be done.

GROW WITH THE FAMILY

Unless you are likely to be making regular and frequent moves, your grand design must take into account your future requirements in five or ten years' time. A toddler's bedroom now will be a teenager's bolt-hole in ten years, and while you redecorate once or twice during that period, it's inadvisable to make large structural changes that won't adapt to teenage living later on.

A diminishing family beyond the teen years is another consideration. Think twice before embarking on costly, permanent projects like second – even third – bathrooms, when a more easily removable shower cabinet in the corner of a bedroom might serve the purpose just as well. On the other hand, if an elderly parent is likely to move in as the youngsters move out, it is well worth the time, trouble and cost to provide the extra, permanent facilities. The same

A well-planned room can cater successfully to the changing needs and tastes of a growing family. This small bedroom assumes a quite different character when it progresses from a young child's room to a teenager's bedroom-cum-study, and yet the changes are purely in the details.

might well apply if you're planning to move when the youngsters leave home, thereby selling an up-graded house and adding to your overall profit.

If you have ever moved from a brand new house to a period property, bringing with you stark hi-tech furniture and bright furnishings in primary colours, you will know just how out of key your possessions can look in their new surroundings. A skilful designer can 'change' the period of the house, but be cautious if you're thinking in terms of the structure. The message here is that if restructuring tampers with the period of a house, it must be done very cleverly, if at all. Tread carefully.

While altering a period house by structural means can be nothing short of heresy, it should be possible to introduce a 'period' feel through our furnishings and decoration. We can successfully give the same room any number of different looks with our choice of wallcoverings, paints, fabrics and style of furniture. Just visit the living rooms in a row of identical houses: You will be amazed how different each can be – perhaps one a cottagey look, another with a Victorian feel, another with a positively surrealist touch of ultra-modernism. All that has happened is that they have taken on the taste and personality of the people who live there. Individuality. That's what it is all about.

OLD FOLKS AT HOME

Very different demands are made on the household that includes an elderly parent. While wishing to remain independent, many old people have simply reached a stage when they are unable to go on living alone. It is not easy to draw together these two opposing needs. The ideal solution is to provide totally separate accommodation within the complex of the home. This will mean that they are able to continue doing things for themselves, but the family is always reassuringly on hand if help is needed, or should some kind of emergency occur.

It might be possible to add on a small purpose-built extension with its own front door, but with easy access to and from the main house. Alternatively, if this is not possible, one or two rooms could be converted into a granny flat – preferably on the ground floor since climbing the stairs could prove difficult.

These rooms should be arranged so they provide a comfortable living room with simple cooking facilities, a bedroom and shower.

If only one room is available, it could be transformed into a bed-sitter with one of the remarkable new sofa beds that are easy to convert, and comfortable. Look out for one of the excellent mini kitchens available that, within the space of a single sink and drainer unit, will provide additional cupboard storage space and a refrigerator. Then, with the addition of a small two-ring cooker, and a microwave oven, kitchen facilities are provided within very little space.

A shower cabinet could be considered for a corner of the room, or if this is quite impossible, consider fitting one in a convenient cranny under the stairs, or converting a small cloakroom into a shower room. Obviously, it's necessary to fit out a shower with accessories suitable for elderly people; the most important items include a non-slip mat in the shower tray, a thermostatically controlled spray, seats, and a good, strong hand grip.

Install a separate telephone so that your elderly parent can still make contact with old friends. And put in some kind of buzzer alarm so that help can be raised quickly if they should fall or become ill.

Planning a room to maximise space is crucial. Even a small room, such as a particularly compact kitchen, may be able to accommodate that kitchen table you have always yearned for. The answer may simply be to resist the temptation to install too many units.

Other safety points to remember:

* When stairs are to be used, make sure that they are well lit and that good sturdy hand rails are provided. If stairs are inevitable, but a major problem, investigate the electronically-controlled chairs that can take a disabled person up and down.
* Door handles should be easy to use, and the doorway will have to be wide enough to allow someone with a wheelchair or walking frame to pass through.
* In the kitchen, make sure a gas cooker has a flame failure device, and that the controls of any type of cooker are easy to operate by an old person with, say, arthritic hands.
* Worktops should be of the right height for someone working from a wheelchair.

Local authorities are usually quite keen to make sure that the old people in their area are well provided for and, if you are planning to convert your home to take in an elderly parent, will listen to your problems with a sympathetic ear. So don't be afraid to go and have a chat with them; they could well tell you about certain services for old people that you didn't know of previously.

LIGHT SHOW

If you have ever been to see one of those amazing laser light shows you will be under no illusion about what one can achieve with light. While I would not suggest that you build in the means to give one of these spectacular displays at home, the balletic and colourful effects may well inspire you to think very carefully about the lighting effects you want for your own rooms.

The main choices lie in atmospheric lighting, and in providing light exactly where you need it; carefully angled lamps, say, when you want to create a study area within a living room, or near an armchair to create a good spot for reading. With clever use of lamps and permanently sited ceiling or wall fittings, you can make the same room seem bright and cheery, or heavy with mood and atmosphere. Part of the room can be phased back into a dim light, leaving other areas highlighted or – if you really wanted to – you could do a fair imitation of Piccadilly Circus!

The most important thing is to make sure you always have light where you want and need it. It does nothing for you – least of all for your eyes – if your desire for moody effects blinds you to the need for a good light to see by.

The best way to decide upon the effects you want is to try them out. Temporarily position spotlights or lamps in varying places in the room. Change the angles about this way and that, and you will see the variety of ways the light catches fabrics, carpets and wallcoverings and how it makes them appear quite different. It's all a question of taste and preference.

A light dimmer switch will make your permanent light fittings more versatile and you should look out for tinted bulbs that can change the mood of a room.

Soft and soothing should be the aim for lighting in a bedroom; a wonderful opportunity to play around with dimmers, tinted bulbs and other effects. Remember, the warmest effect can be achieved with a pink-tinted bulb. Blue, green, yellow, red, for example, will create all kinds of other dramatic moods.

In the kitchen, lighting needs to be good. Choose a striplight placed in a central position for general lighting – a tinted strip is less harsh to the eyes – and for key work positions around the

Adaptability is the keynote for one-room living. As well as convertible furniture such as the popular sofa-bed, the room needs a decorative style that will make it feel as much at home as a bedroom as it does as living area.

kitchen, place small strips or spots to provide local light to the surface in question. These can be switched on and off as necessary.

The essential rule for bathroom lighting is to make sure that it is absolutely safe. Within the bathroom, the light should be switched on only by a safety pullcord and the fitting itself should not be positioned so that it can be handled by wet hands.

WHAT FITTINGS?

Many people will not give house room to wall-light fittings, or ceiling fitments, preferring to light with a series of carefully placed lamps. There is something to be said for having a combination of both. This way you will have complete freedom of choice whatever the mood or circumstance. The style of fitting you choose is obviously a matter of personal preference, but if you can visit a number of stores with a good reputation for their lighting, you will get a better idea of the multitude of designs available to you – from the traditional, Victorian, or cottagey pieces, through to hi-tech designs.

The use of the standard lamp seems to be less in fashion these days, but I believe it can still play a part in the general scheme of things by offering an attractive means of varying the light levels in a room. Placed behind an armchair, for example, it is of exactly the right height to read by.

STORAGE

If you like to 'keep everything in its place', you will need an awful lot of storage space to achieve that ambition! I doubt if it is ever possible to have too much storage space, since we all seem to have a remarkable propensity for filling to the gunwales every spare centimetre we have the luck to acquire.

Just consider what it is like to move house with the mountains of bits and pieces that need storing away, and to find when you get to your new abode that, not only did the previous owners have very different ideas about the amount of storage needed, but that the free-standing items you're taking with you don't fit in anyway. It is likely that you will have to rethink how you are going to find a home for everything, so if any new furniture is to be bought at this

Always be on the lookout for useful spaces that might otherwise be wasted.

stage, try to ensure that it provides extra stowage places.

Plan out exactly what you need for the whole house, room by room. Make a list of everything you have to put in, on – even under – something. Then at least you have a clear picture of how much, and what kind of, storage space you need to provide.

In the living and dining rooms, for example, you will probably want to keep china and cutlery, drinks and glasses, table linen perhaps, books, TV, radio, audio equipment and maybe a video recorder. You'll need storage for records, cassettes or compact discs . . . and that's for starters. You'll also have other personal items for which you must find a home. Investigate the numerous storage systems suitable for living and dining areas; simple open rack shelving in discreet melt-into-the-background finishes or in bold primary colours that are intended to catch the eye. Glass-fronted cabinets allow ornamental possessions to be attractively displayed without becoming a target for dust – and precious pieces are less likely to get broken the fewer times you have to dust them.

Electronic home-entertainment equipment can be fitted on to shelf units or into cabinets with doors that close it away from view when not in use. Expensive equipment is best away from the prying eyes of passing burglars – who are adept at spotting the green glow emitted by many video recorders through an uncurtained window. Many stereo systems, these days, come as neat, stacked packages that look well on a shelf system, but for those who have the rather larger, separate pieces of equipment, they are probably more neatly stored inside a cabinet.

SPACE-MAKERS

The problem with shelves is that they normally have uprights or brackets which, at the best of times, can hardly be described as beautiful. So the one-component shelf-support system called Cliffhanger is a clever idea which is worthy of the Design Council label on the DIY packaging.

The old-style sideboards seem to be re-emerging and can be seen in the latest furniture brochures alongside the wall unit systems that will also provide storage for china and cutlery. You are expected to build up these wall systems from units purpose-built with drawers and cupboards as well as open shelving; simply choose the units you need – and can fit in.

In the living room, or in a separate study, a desk can be an attractive addition while still performing its practical role. Many of the latest desks will also provide stowage space for computer and screen. And consider the ever-useful bureau with all kinds of pigeon holes for important papers.

In the bedroom, the bed itself can give you a large storage area for blankets, pillows and linen. Look for under-bed drawers that pull out to reveal a surprisingly large amount of space.

It's not easy to do without a wardrobe (impossible you might think, but friends of mine did survive six years with only a fashion rail and an inordinate number of shoes lined up under the window!). So whether you opt for a custom-built-in system, a converted existing cupboard or one of the free-standing wardrobes that, like the sideboard, seem to be returning to favour, you should sit down and plan out your requirements before you buy anything.

Cool blue can bring a heightened sense of space to a room – enhanced by unfussy furnishings and a minimum of clutter. Here, the storage unit could hardly be simpler, yet it makes a real contribution to the room's overall style.

Just because a room is large, there is no obligation to try and fill it up with furniture. Here, the sparseness of furnishing capitalises on the spaciousness of the room – to dramatic effect.

A large range of purpose-built wardrobe units are now available where the manufacturer will send a planner to measure up and advise, then supply and fit the complete unit. These can often have just the amount of hanging space that you require, or drawers, shoe racks, shelves – even wire 'drawers' that pull out on runners. They are simply designed to fit the available space, and fitted out inside as required.

Children's bedrooms in particular are especially suited to the built-in bunk and unit fitments that can be bought. So that, coupled with bedside cabinets and chests of drawers, the bedroom is particularly well served with storage fitments. More about bedrooms in Chapter 9.

OUT OF SIGHT

Further space can be found under stairs, on landings (usually where an airing cupboard can be found), and in the loft . . . specially useful this, since rarely used items can be tucked away safely out of view. Do take care, though, that access to services in the roof space is not impeded; you'll not be amused if you have to scramble among a heap of boxes to reach a burst pipe.

Under-the-stairs provides a neat space for all kinds of treatment. Perhaps you can build in a cupboard, or an under-stairs office with desk fitment and filing drawers, a display cabinet; even a pretty pine chest – good to look at, with drawer space thrown in. Or you could construct a special area with hanging space for coats, racks for outdoor shoes and wellies, umbrellas, golf clubs, cycling gear or skates.

The kitchen and bathroom are specially important when considering adequate storage space. These areas are covered thoroughly in chapters 7 and 8.

Ingenious furniture can provide generous storage space in all sorts of places.

Storage in style: shelving can be a decorative part of any scheme as well as a practical one. Colour-matched with the skirting, picture-rail, cornice and table in this room, the storage units become an integral part of the overall theme.

There are a number of clever storage aids that cannot be classified as pieces of furniture as such, but certainly serve an additional and helpful role in the struggle to keep things in their place. Look out for the unusual Beeline Honeycomb units with shelves in most of the hexagonal compartments. Good for a child's room or for a teenager, they come in white with trim in bright primary colours. There's also an attractive range of storage cubes providing cupboard and drawer space: again in white and primary colours.

Additionally you can create your own storage ideas with a little ingenuity. A number of wicker baskets can be painted in your room's accent colour and placed on an old round saucepan rack, also smartened up with paint to match. Old box files that have seen better days can be renovated with an adhesive plastic, or covered with a wallpaper that matches – or contrasts – with the wallcovering used in the room. Two or three-tiered plastic storage boxes can be stacked then topped with a hardboard 'table' top and covered with a pretty flowered cloth – it can be dismantled in a moment to get at the contents.

A convenient office space built into a spare bedroom makes double use of a room that might otherwise be wasted.

HOME COMMUNICATIONS

The greatest technical advances to affect our day-to-day lives at home have surely been those recently made in the field of domestic appliances and communications. We look at domestic appliances in chapter 7, but what of communications? The way we can communicate with each other has been revolutionised by the introduction of cassettes and video film, video cameras and recorders, and the sophisticated equipment on which we can play back the results.

Our televisions can have Prestel and Teletext facilities which enable us to call on a vast fund of useful information, and additionally make it possible to perform all manner of tiresome chores without stirring from our armchairs. If shopping from home is what you desire most, now you can and your bank balance can be adjusted, too, without your having to step inside a bank.

The other revolution in the field of communications lies in the not-so-humble telephone. If our grandparents – even our parents – had been told that before the century was out we would be using on a day-by-day basis telephones that have memories and re-call facilities; that some would include a 'secrecy' button; that others will incorporate a three-wave-band radio and 12-hour digital clock, they would surely have found it hard to believe. Nor could they have imagined that we could answer calls from the garden or workshop using a cordless telephone. Many of us already own such wonders in our homes.

As well as renting, phones can now be purchased – from a number of dealers. Indeed, you can now buy telephones from several of the large high street

Today's telephone equipment is neat and compact, making little demand on space.

A storage system can serve as a dramatic focal point for a room, especially as a display area for fine *objets*.

stores where they are displayed on shelves like any other commodity. Not all models are manufactured by BT, but if purchasing one of the others, check that it has the green circle of the British Approvals Board for Telecommunications (BABT) approval. A red triangle means it is *not* approved, and British Telecom are within their rights to disconnect it from their system.

If you don't like missing a single call – or if it is vital in the business sense – a telephone answering machine will have you wondering why you didn't install one before. Just insert a cassette, make sure it is switched on, then record a message for any callers asking them to leave their name, number and a short message. Then off you go content in the knowledge that you will know exactly who called you while you were out. It is possible to have a voice-activated remote control device that will allow you to call in to your own number to receive any messages.

It is surprisingly simple to install a complete telephone system within the house, either by putting telephones into each key room – *every* room if you wish – or by installing a number of sockets throughout the house in order to 'plug in' wherever you go. You could trot round with the cordless phone in your pocket if you've a mind to! And with a large number of stylish models and colours to choose from you can match the telephone into the decorative style of the room.

IN STYLE

Whatever kind of house you live in, or style of decor you prefer, you will find there is storage furniture to suit your particular taste.

Modern, clean-cut and very hi-tech; middle of the road; traditional; reproduction. All can be found in furniture stores throughout the country. But if, even with this variety of choice you still can't see exactly what you want, take a look at small antique and junk shops or attend local auctions where it is possible to pick up attractive pieces in need of renovation. Cupboards, chests, blanket boxes, dressers – any of these, once restored, could well fit in handsomely with the rest of your scheme and provide valuable extra storage into the bargain.

HEATING

When the heat's on – as it usually has to be for at least half the year – you should be sure you're getting all the warmth you're paying for

The long and bitter winters of recent years have made it very plain to most of us just how vital an effective home heating system is. And high fuel prices – whose continued inflation has been only marginally interrupted by the plummet in crude oil rates – act as constant reminder of just how vital an *efficient* heating set-up is, too.

Four out of five family homes in Britain have some kind of central heating, so the chances are that the house or flat you are about to improve or move into is already equipped. The chances are also pretty good that the system, if more than five or ten years old, will be in need of attention, improvement or even replacement.

HOW CENTRAL HEATING WORKS

To most of us, a 'wet' system – namely one which functions by having heated water circulated around circuits of radiators – is an indecipherable jumble of pipes, valves and curious electrically operated controls. The whole thing is a matter of interest only when (a) it starts making strange noises, or springs leaks or (b) when the boiler won't light or the radiators don't heat up even when the boiler does or (c) when a flabbergastingly enormous fuel bill arrives for the first winter quarter – and there's still another quarter to come!

In view of these common heating hazards, it makes sense to know a little of how the system works – and of how you can keep it going, at the most reasonable possible cost.

The boiler

At the heart of the system is the boiler, powered by gas (either piped in by British Gas or from a Calor bulk tank), oil or a solid fuel. From one side of the boiler, two pipes emerge. One, usually the upper, is the 'flow' pipe which carries the heated water to the circuits. Close to the boiler, a pump is fitted, usually into this pipe, to force the hot water round at a rapid rate, ensuring it reaches the radiators before it loses too much heat. The lower pipe is the 'return', carrying the cooled water back into the boiler for reheating.

From the other side of the boiler, another two pipes emerge. The lower one is the supply from the water tank, better known as the 'feed and expansion' tank. The upper pipe is the 'expansion' one – up which heated water naturally rises by gravity (hot water being lighter than cold) to the hot water cylinder which supplies the hot taps in the house. In effect, a branch from the expansion pipe carries the hot water through a coil immersed in the cylinder, thus heating up the cold water which is supplied to the cylinder from the main cold tank (the bigger one, which is separate from the feed and expansion tank). This coil is connected at its return end to the cold feed, thus forming a complete circuit from boiler to cylinder and back again. This is known as the 'primary' circuit.

The expansion pipe has another function, for it rises straight up from the boiler to the feed and expansion tank,

The many rural homes and communities which lie out of reach of a gas main can now enjoy the comfort and convenience of gas heating – and cooking – from a bulk tank on their own property.

Today's central heating boilers are extremely compact. Gas boilers, and some oil-fired models, can be tucked into a kitchen, either freestanding or wall-hung, with the 'balanced' flue passing through the wall behind to a grille on the outside. Many models are made to fit neatly in with a run of floor or wall units.

over which it curves to a position just above the tank. In effect, this forms a safety guarantee for the boiler, because should the flow of water to the radiators and/or cylinder be blocked and the boiler kept on running, it would ultimately blow up. With the expansion pipe to carry the heated water back to the tank, this is prevented. The height of the pipe is calculated, of course, so the hot water will only rise to its full length if boiler pressure is abnormally high.

Pipework

The flow pipe from the boiler to the radiators is branched into two or more circuits – usually for upstairs and downstairs – to keep the length of pipework to the furthest radiator within

As well as all sorts of sizes, radiators come in a diverse range of shapes. This coolly elegant model (it's the tall item to the left of the picture, in case you couldn't spot it!) gives the lie to the idea that all radiators look the same.

reasonable limits. In a large house, there may be two circuits for each floor.

The best modern central heating systems are designed with two pipes serving the radiators. One is the 'flow' which delivers the heated water at one end of the radiator; the other is the 'return' into which the cooled water runs from the radiator's opposite end. This means that the hot 'flow' stays hot, rather than being cooled by the water escaping from the radiators along the circuit – so even the radiator at the furthest point away from the boiler receives a properly heated supply.

Radiators

Manufactured in a host of different shapes and sizes, with single or double panels, radiators are simply compact

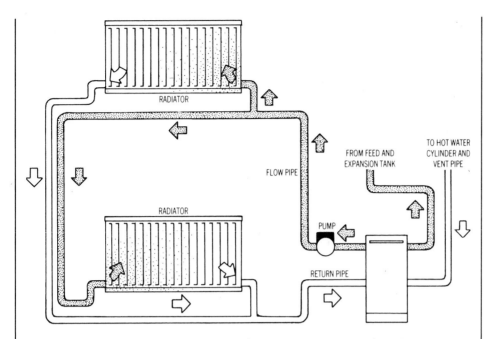

RADIATOR

RADIATOR

FLOW PIPE

FROM FEED AND
EXPANSION TANK

TO HOT WATER
CYLINDER AND
VENT PIPE

PUMP

RETURN PIPE

Today's central heating systems employ the two-pipe method of circulating hot water. One pipe carries the water from the boiler to the radiators. A separate pipe returns the cooled water to the boiler. This means that the hot water remains hot and heats up the radiators furthest from the boiler just as well as it does those nearest.

water tanks with a valve at each end. The flow valve admits the water and the return valve is set to allow the cooled water to trickle out at a rate which makes optimum use of the heat before allowing the water to escape into the return pipe. The return valve is referred to as a 'lockshield' type because it is locked into its set position by the installer. So you can turn the plastic cap as much as you like, and it will not alter the setting. To turn the radiator off, therefore, you simply close down the flow valve – which effectively has two positions: on and off.

In a properly designed heating system, the radiators for each room should be of sufficient capacity – rated in British Thermal Units (Btu) – to warm the room to the 'design' temperature. The amount of heat needed for the room depends on its size and on the construction of the walls, floor and ceiling, plus what lies on the far side of those walls and above and below the room. A heating engineer therefore takes into consideration such items as whether the walls are external, how much window area there is, and whether there is a heated room below or not.

Most radiators are positioned under windows because they combat the natural down draught from the glass. The space beneath a window is also convenient, and could probably not be put to any other use. One more merit for the window position is that the staining evident on walls from radiators' heat is avoided.

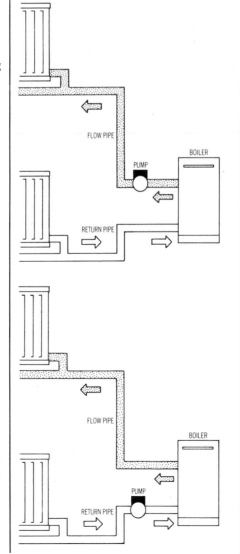

FLOW PIPE

PUMP

BOILER

RETURN PIPE

FLOW PIPE

BOILER

PUMP

RETURN PIPE

It is the action of the pump, forcing the water rapidly around the circuits, that makes heating with small-bore pipes possible. The pump is usually set on the flow pipe, close to the boiler; this way, it pushes the water around the system. If positioned on the return pipe (lower picture), the pump is, in effect, pulling the water around – less ideal as this can cause air to get into the system.

Radiators don't *have* to go under windows. This one, controlled by its own thermostatic radiator valve, is well placed, because if it had been behind the full-length curtains a lot of its heat would be lost directly through the window. And the thermostatic valve's efficiency would be reduced by any draughts circulating behind the curtains.

A major drawback of the window position occurs if you hang full-length curtains over the radiator. The warm air trapped behind will escape in wasteful quantities through the glass. If you must have curtains that reach the floor, think about positioning the radiators somewhere else, or double-glazing the window.

Controls

A heating system is really only as good as its controls, and in many cases the performance of an existing set-up can be improved dramatically by updating these controls.

Systems are all too often equipped only with an on-off switch and time clock plus a single room thermostat which can be set to switch the boiler and pump on and off according to when its sensor detects temperature changes. These very basic controls have numerous, fuel-wasting disadvantages, and in all likelihood should be replaced – or at least supplemented – as a matter of priority.

The drawbacks of a simple time clock are threefold. One is that you have no separate control over the heating and hot water – they are either both on or both off. The second is that a time clock will allow just two pairs of settings per day.

The third is that the clock merely instructs the boiler to switch on and off – it cannot be operated in conjunction with a thermostat when off.

Programmers

Good heating systems today are controlled by a device called a 'programmer' which permits several on-off settings in each 24 hours, and also provides separate controls for heating and hot water. An advanced type of programmer called a 'modulating controller' goes further by not simply switching the system on and off, but by maintaining a carefully controlled temperature in the continuously circulating water. This means that the house is never allowed to go completely cold – and thus that the boiler does not have to run full tilt every time it comes on again in order to reheat the fabric of the building.

The virtues of a modulating controller are obvious and the fuel-savings it makes can be dramatic. But it is an expensive device to buy and install, complete with its heat-loss sensors. Nevertheless, one major manufacturer claims that the initial cost will be recouped through fuel economies inside three years.

THERMOSTATS

Such a controller obviates the need for a room thermostat. Where a thermostat is necessary – namely with a standard programmer – its position is all-important. In a small house or flat the thermostat can be installed in the most-used room, well away from any source of local heat such as an open fire or of local chill such as a doorway from a very draughty hall.

In a home with more than a very few rooms, however, this single thermostat will be insufficient because the conditions prevailing in, say, a living room will be far too variable. For example a south- or west-facing living room will get a certain amount of sunlight each sunny day and the room's raised temperature will make the thermostat switch the whole heating system off – leaving rooms at the opposite side of the house unheated.

One solution is to equip each room with its own thermostat, in the shape of special thermostatic valves on each radiator. These are fitted in place of the hand valves that control the inflow of water, and have a range of settings; when the radiator reaches the set temperature, the valve closes down – and saves much wasted heat in bedrooms during the day, in rooms where sunlight makes heat needless and in other places where just a little 'background' heat is called for most of the time.

If you are having central heating installed, it is well worth considering having these valves fitted – as their installation cost should be no greater than for standard valves. Having them fitted on to all the radiators on an existing system, on the other hand, could prove costly in plumber's bills as it is often necessay to adjust pipework to accommodate thermostatic valves' different dimensions. Ask your plumber for an estimate before you rush out to buy any valves – as the labour charge may well eclipse even the cost of the materials!

You *may* be able to replace your standard valves with thermostatic ones yourself if you can find a model that exactly matches the dimensions of your existing valves, in which case resetting the plumbing won't be necessary. Make a note of your valves' make and model number and ask the plumber's merchant, or the customer service department of the thermostatic valve manufacturer, whether the models they offer will correspond.

OTHER CONTROLS

Just as it is sensible to have separate time-switch controls for heating and hot water, so it makes sense to have separate temperature controls for each. As a rule, boilers are designed to heat the water destined for the radiators to 82 degrees

Where curtains are only sill-length and space under a window is short, a long, double-panelled radiator makes a very efficient and unobtrusive answer.

centigrade, but this sort of temperature is quite unnecessary for tap water. So to avoid wasting fuel heating a cylinderful of water to this high – even scalding – level, you should fit a cylinder-thermostat valve which will close down the flow to the cylinder when its contents reach the maximum heat needed for tap water, namely 60 degrees C.

This type of control cannot, unfortunately, be fitted to a cylinder supplied by a solid fuel boiler. This is because the cylinder provides a 'heat sink' for the boiler's output when demand at the radiators for hot water is low. Because a solid fuel boiler cannot simply be switched on and off – as gas and oil appliances can – the primary circuit to the cylinder must always be left open to prevent the boiler overheating.

Another control which can be indispensable – again only with a gas- or oil-fired system – is a 'frost thermostat' which automatically switches the boiler on if it detects a temperature close to freezing. If your boiler is in an outhouse, for example, this device may well save you from the disastrous consequences of a burst pipe.

One more useful control: the 'zone valve'. This is a means of giving separate control to different circuits of radiators, so that for example you can have your upstairs and downstairs heating operating on their own time clocks. These valves are motorised, so can operate automatically.

STARTING FROM SCRATCH

If you are installing a complete new central heating system, there are a number of important decisions to take before seeking quotations for the work.

The first decision is which fuel to use. Most households, particularly those in urban areas, have access to gas, which is unquestionably the most convenient fuel – as well as being very competitive in price with solid fuels and far cheaper than oil. If your home is not already connected to a gas supply, check with your local British Gas office to see whether your property is within 25 yards of a main – in which case you are entitled to be connected.

A gas-fired boiler, even of a capacity to heat a large house, will fit comfortably into a kitchen, and will not need a

chimney. The 'balanced flue' terminal simply passes through an external wall to an unobtrusive grille on the other side. Today's boilers are surprisingly silent-running, and many are designed to blend in with kitchen units – either freestanding or wall-mounted. Pipework and pump can be concealed inside an adjacent unit.

Where gas is not available, you can ask British Gas for a quotation for the cost of connecting you to the nearest supply (namely one that is more than 25 yards away). But if the distance is more than a few yards you are likely to find this cost prohibitive.

The alternatives are solid fuel, oil or liquefied petroleum gas (LPG). Solid fuel boilers are necessarily bulkier than gas models, and of course require regular fuelling – at least once a day – and cleaning. And a proper chimney will be called for too, as solid fuel

burners cannot be vented by balanced flue. You will also need somewhere to store the necessary fuel which, unlike gas, must be paid for in advance (preferably in the summer, when very generous discounts are offered by coal merchants).

Solid fuel boilers can, happily, have their attractions as well as their obvious disadvantages. There are now some very handsome stoves on the market which, fitted with a spacious 'back boiler' behind, can power several radiators plus a hot-water supply – all in addition to providing an attractive focal point in a living room. Many such stoves burn all manner of fuels from wood to a variety of coal types – though to power a central heating system, they usually perform best on quality fuels such as anthracite or furnacite.

Solid fuels score well on economy – rivalling gas and of course incurring no standing charges for their use. The same cannot be said of oil, the heating variety of which (namely diesel) has not dropped in price to the domestic consumer by anything like the percentage its crude form has.

Oil boilers do have many of the advantages of gas. They have similar controllability; they can now be fitted with balanced flues; they can be amazingly compact. But they do tend to be much noisier – and of course they need to be supplied from a large storage tank. Partly because they are manufactured in much lower volume than gas appliances, oil boilers are substantially more expensive.

Comparable in fuel-cost terms with oil is the LPG-powered boiler. Most major manufacturers now produce appliances to run on LPG – which is supplied from a bulk tank lent to the customer by Calor (so you don't have to pay for the tank, as you must for oil).

Apart from the aforementioned advantages of gas boilers, an LPG supply also enables households not connected to a mains supply – and that goes for some two million British homes – to cook by gas.

CHOOSING AN INSTALLER

Once you know which fuel you will run your heating on, you can invite two or three estimates for the cost of installing the system. Your local British Gas office will be pleased to quote for the work, or you can call in a national company. You are likely to get a very competitive quote from your local heating specialist or plumber – but do check their credentials. For a gas installation, the contractor should be registered with the Confederation for the Registration of Gas Installers (CORGI) – which means he is approved in the gas industry as a competent installer.

For all kinds of gas appliances, it is advisable to choose installers with membership of one of the recognised trade associations. Their work is carried out to specified standards, and is guaranteed as such.

HEAT WITHOUT RADIATORS

Not all central heating systems rely on radiators. Some houses, for example, have built-in heating in the form of ducts passing under floors and through hollow

Some central heating boilers are more glamorous than others! Running on traditional solid fuel, oil or gas, an Aga can power several radiators as well as providing hot water and cooking.

A log-burning stove can not only look good; the best models produce great amounts of heat and can be economical on fuel. Some stoves can be fitted with a back-boiler to supply hot water and even power a circuit of radiators.

walls, carrying warm air from a central heat emitter to grilles in the walls and floors of each room. Two problems with these systems are that they are difficult to control, and they are virtually impossible to install in an existing building.

One system that claims to overcome these problems is the Swedish-pioneered underfloor method which uses polyethylene pipe to carry heated water to all parts of the house. The system, marketed in Britain by Wirsbo (UK) Ltd, can be run on any type of fuel and great claims are made for its economy and effectiveness – as well as for the fact that it employs no space-hogging and unsightly radiators, of course!

HEATING BY ELECTRICITY

Storage heating systems, which are composed of a circuit of electric radiators wired to a special meter, are claimed to be an economic form of home heating. The basis of this claim is that by 'storing' heat which is generated by half-price electricity between 11 pm and 6 am (on the 'Economy 7' tariff) and then gradually emitting that warmth through the day, the radiators can keep the property at a comfortable temperature round the clock.

In a home with particularly good thermal insulation – namely with very thick solid walls or insulation-filled cavity walls, draught-free doors and windows plus very thoroughly insulated floors and ceilings – it is possible that the storage system will perform adequately. But in a less prodigiously wrapped-up house, there is likely to be a pretty chill spell from late afternoon until 11 pm – which is, unfortunately, exactly the time most members of the household are likely to be home!

Of course, it is no problem to turn the radiators on at such a time – but the cost of the heat, at full tariff, can be very high. It should be said, however, that storage systems are significantly cheaper to install than 'wet' ones – and that today's storage radiators are very much slimmer and more attractive than their ponderous forbears were. Controls have improved, too, so that heat output can be restrained quite successfully until it is needed.

Storage heaters are unlikely to suit a detached house, but for a small terraced home or a flat they can provide a useful and undeniably economic alternative to central heating – particularly if boosted by individual room heaters such as open fires.

HEATING ROOM BY ROOM

There is only one economic method of heating a whole house, and that is by a central system. Individual gas, electric or solid fuel fires are uneconomic at the best of times, and heating a whole house with them would probably ruin you!

But there is no denying the charm of an open fireplace with its own fire. And such a fire *can* be a useful source of heat for the room itself, and perhaps even for the rest of the house. There are a large number of gas and solid fuel appliances which consist of attractive stoves or fires with back-boilers fitted behind. These boilers can be rated as high as 45,000 Btu – which, some makers claim, can supply up to 10 radiators.

For a fire that is simply a fire, your choice is between electricity, gas and solid fuel, though you need a flue for the latter two. For a gas fire, a good new idea is Thorn EMI's Thru flue type, which needs no chimney but simply fits through the wall behind.

If you have a chimney, a 'real' fire can be attractive and economic. Today's smokeless fuels mean you can enjoy a real fire wherever you live, either in the form of a stove or as a simple grate. To make sure you get some real heat from your fireplace, ask the local branch of the Solid Fuel Advisory Service for the names of specialist suppliers and installers in your area, who will be able not only to supply you with the best stove or grate for your needs but to advise you on your chimney and how – as is often necessary – you can improve its draught, and thus the effectiveness of your fire.

INSULATION

Just as it is vital to insulate your home, it is vital to insulate your heating system too. Start with the hot water cylinder. Many of today's new cylinders come ready-insulated, but if yours lacks any kind of jacket, you should fit one straightaway. Choose a jacket that matches the model number of your cylinder, and ensure that it conforms with the appropriate British Standard – no. 5615.

A decorative focal point in any room, a real fire with a back-boiler fitted out of sight behind can warm all of your home. Highly fuel-efficient, and simple to fill and clear of ash, today's solid-fuel appliances are an attractive option for heating systems.

You should protect all pipework that passes through unheated spaces. This prevents heat loss in cellars, lofts, understairs and so on. And it can save you from the horrors of frozen – and possibly burst – pipes in very cold conditions, too. Lagging pipes is made very simple with the specially moulded plastic foam tubings now widely available from DIY centres and builders' merchants. When buying these products, do be careful to choose the right size for the pipes concerned as they are moulded to fit the varying widths of pipe in common use – namely 15 mm, 22 mm and 28 mm.

To prevent unnecessary heat loss through the feed and expansion tank in the loft, insulate this by tying slabs of expanded polystyrene or sections of glass-fibre blanket to the sides. Make a plywood lid for the top, and cover that with insulation material too. Do not put any insulation material under the tank, as the heat escaping from the warm room below should prevent the water freezing.

It makes sense to insulate the main water tank, too, by the same means, again leaving the space below uninsulated. This will not only prevent a freeze-up, but can help to keep the water temperature up – and thus make it cheaper in fuel terms to heat in the cylinder.

Coal-effect and log-effect fires have come a long way in terms both of looks and effectiveness in room-heating.

KITCHENS

Despite the incredible changes that have taken place in the way the average family lives, the kitchen remains the hub of the home. Indeed, we increasingly regard it as the all purpose room – the very heart of todays modern families.

Fewer women may be performing the traditional stay-at-home role than in the past, but the kitchen has evolved into an activity area for the whole family, where the man of the house is more than likely to take his turn at cooking the evening meal or preparing for a dinner party. And he'll be found performing other kitchen-based activities.

This change of emphasis means that it is more important than ever to plan a new kitchen with special care, making sure that you cater for your particular lifestyle. For a family of four – all working, all taking meals at different times of the day – will make entirely different demands on a kitchen than a family with a home-based member ready to look after the needs of the rest.

Other factors to consider involve time and money. Do you have the time – or inclination – to do the work yourself? Indeed, can you afford *not* to? If it is to be a DIY number, how do you go about it? Can a well-fitted kitchen be installed for a low budget? Can you get a home improvement loan in order to have a luxury kitchen installed for you?

Make sure you have all these things clearly sorted out in your mind before you start to make any decisions.

THE WAY YOU LIVE

'Lifestyle' seems to be the buzz word of the eighties, but it exactly describes in the modern vernacular what we need to know about ourselves. Unless your kitchen can be tailor made to the way you and your family live, you'll find that it never really works for *you*.

To discover those needs, jot down in a notebook, all the functions you expect of your kitchen and the needs of the other people who will be using it. Try answering these questions as you go, and you will begin to build up a total picture:

* How many people will use the kitchen?
* How many will be using it at the same time?
* How tall are they?
* Will it also be used as a living/dining room?
* Are there small children in the family?
* Will you entertain friends there?
* Do you have pets?

See how your answers have established several facts already?

If lots of people will use the kitchen, it needs to be as large as possible. Small kitchens can be enlarged – sometimes by simply rehanging a door to swing outwards, or by installing a sliding door – but you might have to consider extending the kitchen with a purpose-built extension. Consider, too, the possibility of converting a larger dining room into a large kitchen/diner and making your small, existing kitchen a utility room.

The heights of the people who will be using the kitchen is important. Units come in standard heights for average people, and these are not always good or comfortable for those who are small or

Not just a kitchen, but a family room, too, this is one in which it would be a pleasure to spend time. The hand-painted wooden units bring a warm and friendly feel to the room.

very tall, and so they have to be adjusted – either by raising them on blocks, or by planing a little from the base of all floor-standing units. But be sure what is the required height before you do this! What if a very tiny woman has to work alongside a very tall man? In this case it is best to design the kitchen in such a way that it provides work surfaces at heights suitable for both people.

For a living/dining area, space must be left for table and chairs to be placed comfortably so that it is still possible to move around the kitchen without bumping into, or tripping over, objects and people. For entertaining, the surroundings need to be discreet with adjustable lighting that will focus on the table while the rest of the kitchen can be subdued with a dimmer switch. Be cautious about using a kitchen/diner for entertaining if you are not a tidy cook and find it hard to clear up as you go. Otherwise you can forget your elegant surroundings – it'll be more like eating in a scene from Dante's *Inferno*.

As for children and pets, both need catering for in their way. Small children will grab out at anything within reach, so 'think safe' and remember to use safety locks, child-proof covers to sockets, and a cooker guard to protect them from boiling pans. Pets that both eat and sleep in the kitchen need a quiet corner where they can remain undisturbed.

When you consider the actual cooking, jot down notes about it in the same way. First look at these points:
* Does the main cook of the household have a full-time job away from home?
* Are you a great host/hostess?
* Do you batch bake? Cook for the freezer? Make preserves?
* Are freestanding or built-in appliances preferred?

If the main cook, along with the rest of the family, has a full-time job, the kitchen needs to be kitted out for speedy convenience preparation and cooking: a

Kitchens don't often run to these proportions, but when they do they offer the opportunity to create a really stunning effect. The black units give a starkly dramatic look, and yet do not make the room claustrophobic. The appliances are neatly blended in behind matching decor panels.

Not surprisingly, natural wood kitchens have always been popular. In addition to the familiar pine and dark oak, other variations include the light, bright look of this handsome limed oak kitchen.

microwave oven, perhaps; a freezer full of ready meals; other time-saving small appliances such as a pressure cooker.

On the other hand, cooking for a large number of people makes different demands on the kitchen. A cooker with an especially large oven might be called for. So might some large serving dishes and pans – and suitable storage will be necessary for these. Extra storage is needed as well for the special equipment necessary for preserving, batch baking and the preparation and packaging of items destined for the freezer.

As for your choice of freestanding or built-in appliances; that is likely to be simply a question of your personal preference, but it could be that you're anticipating another move in a fairly short time, and would like to be able to take such appliances with you.

HOW MUCH STORAGE?

It is inevitable that we fill to the brim whatever storage space we have – even if it was considered more than ample at the outset. It is equally true that most homes don't provide enough storage space anyway. Especially in the kitchen.

When the size of the kitchen is limited, careful planning is needed to give good stowage, and to make sure that space is not wasted. Many kitchen manufacturers offer storage aids such as wire baskets that slide on runners – wonderful for checking exactly what you have in the cupboard. They can be used for a multitude of purposes from fruit and veg to cans and dried goods, or pots and pans. Other refinements on offer include special racks for cleaning materials, a drop-down concealed ironing board and, specially useful, a carousel that swings the cupboard's contents out into full view as you open the door.

Whether or not you go in for these somewhat expensive purpose-built extras, what is clear is that the equipment stored in your kitchen must be well organised with a place provided for everything. So before you commit yourself to the number and type of units you want, itemise every single thing that needs a home in your kitchen; all the pots and pans, china, cutlery, food and so on. This way you will have a much better picture of the storage space you are likely to need.

Look out for the extra storage facilities offered by some manufacturers. A pull-out cupboard unit provides ample storage in a very small area.

Another ingenious saver of space is the pull-out table top – a boon in small kitchens.

WHAT KITCHEN?

Manufacturers of fitted kitchens produce three kinds:

* Flat pack – the sort you assemble and fit yourself.
* Standard rigid – ready assembled, to be fitted either by a specialist or by yourself.
* Purpose built – the kind that is designed and built specially with your kitchen in mind.

Self assembly

The DIY flat-pack kitchen is the cheapest option, available from DIY Superstores. Companies like Grovewood and Crosby also supply a flat-pack version of their kitchens.

It is simple enough to arrive at one of the DIY stores to make your selection, but that isn't the whole story. Having decided that, yes, you *can* cope with the fairly major task of dismantling your old kitchen and putting in the new one, you must come armed with a precision plan of the floor area with all the units marked (see how on page 90). Measure the depth of appliances before deciding on your required worktop measurement. Some appliances, while apparently being standard in size, actually need more depth to accommodate plumbing and so on. The actual measurement of both units and appliances can be taken from the manufacturers' catalogues.

It is usually possible to make your choice and take the units away with you, so make sure you have adequate transport. Hire a van, if necessary, since not all stores provide a delivery service.

Some stores can offer a planning service and it's a good idea to take full advantage of this if you are in any way a beginner at this game. And if you need advice, don't be afraid to ask.

Look carefully at the display kitchens in stores: are they well constructed, do they look sturdy, do the drawers run smoothly? Are the doors strongly fitted with good hinges? However cheaply you have bought and constructed a kitchen, your patience will wear thin when drawers perpetually stick or the doors fall off when your offspring lean on them – as they will. Before you buy, read through the fitting instructions and make sure you understand them. If you don't, *ask*. If you still don't, buy something else where the instructions can be understood.

Each unit will be packed separately, and will include all its 'fixings'; but when you reach home, check thoroughly that everything that should be there has been included.

Standard Rigid Units

These are sold through specialist kitchen studios, manufacturers' showrooms, or through large department stores such as John Lewis. The kitchens are usually constructed into roomsets so that you can wander round them and have the chance to look at the different ranges on offer. It helps you decide if you can live with them. You will be able to compare the different kinds of materials and colours in which they are constructed, and to judge what would be right in your own kitchen at home.

The choice is huge. Laminates in a multitude of styles and colours. Wood ranges, excessively modern, or traditional. Textured finishes – even a cane finish. But let your final choice be based on your lifestyle.

This is the kitchen you will have to live with for some time. It will not be cheap, and you want to be totally happy with your choice for a good few years ahead.

You will already have decided what storage space you need, but notice the extraordinary range of extra facilities offered by the manufacturers of these kitchens; foldaway ironing tables, larder drawers, carousel door units, pull-down tables. See too the special décor panels designed to fit into the front of certain appliances like fridges and dishwashers, so they melt into the overall scheme of things. The price variations are enormous. It is possible to have an average-sized kitchen fitted for you in a standard rigid range for around £1500 if you choose the bottom of the range model from one of the less-expensive manufacturers. From this basic level, prices can jump in leaps and bounds according to the manufacturer, the units and fitments you choose, and the size of the kitchen. But with a long-term

purchase of this kind, which could well put value on to the price of your house, the expenditure can be deemed to be worth it.

Some companies make a charge for the planning service, refundable when you order the kitchen, which at least deters customers looking just for a plan. Others make no charge at all, like Schreiber, who came up with three different designs and colour schemes for the same kitchen in the Halifax house.

The Purpose-Built Kitchen

These kitchens are made to measure precisely – and individually – to your personal requirements and the demands made by an awkwardly shaped room. It is the crème de la crème: an expensive, beautifully made quality one-off. Depending on what units and which manufacturer you choose, it is possible to start from about £2,000 for an average 10-foot square kitchen, but you can pay several times as much as this if you've a mind to.

For the proficient handyperson, a self-assembly kitchen can mean a great saving. Care must be taken with installation, of course, but it is possible, at a very much reduced cost, to achieve a kitchen as smart as this self-assembly one, trimmed in beech.

A kitchen of this quality becomes a room in which you could happily entertain. Look at the soft relaxing tones in which you work and eat.

SELF-ASSEMBLY KITCHENS

PROS

* ★ Off-the-shelf purchase
* ★ DIY construction
* ★ Low cost
* ★ Wide choice of units
* ★ Large ranges and modern styling of varying qualities
* ★ Some stores offer advice and planning service

CONS

* ★ Major DIY job. If in doubt about time available, or ability, consider employing a local fitter
* ★ Suitable transport needed. Car not really large enough
* ★ If the store will not deliver, you may have to hire a van

WHEN YOU'RE BUYING

* ★ Check display units in store are strong, and fit together neatly
* ★ Check drawers run smoothly
* ★ Check hinges are sturdy
* ★ Ask to see the fitting instructions and make sure you understand them
* ★ Check all fittings come complete
* ★ *Always* make sure that every fitting is in the pack when you get home

PRICE GUIDE

* ★ For 10ft by 10ft kitchen, range from approximately £550 to £1500. More for solid wood

For some people with awkwardly shaped kitchens impossible to fit out with standard units, or who want a degree of individuality, the purpose-built kitchen is the 'total' answer. And for those prepared to invest in it – house values do seem to increase when the kitchen is really special – Halifax home improvement loans are available.

Special finishes are abundant; paint techniques such as murals, *trompe l'oeil*, as well as the simpler effects, Antique finished, acid etching, stained glass,

STANDARD RIGID KITCHENS

PROS

* Fits most kitchens
* Ready assembled
* Vast choice
* Free planning advice
* Large range of extras
* Five-year warranty possible

CONS

* Will cost more than flat pack
* Several weeks' delivery likely

WHEN YOU'RE BUYING

* Spend time looking at products from several manufacturers and check out exactly what you are getting for your money
* Visit showrooms and kitchen centres and inspect the units carefully
* Look at home styling magazines for latest concepts you might like incorporated
* Choose a range that will not date
* Make sure the kitchen incorporates what *you* want, not what the planner thinks you want

PRICE GUIDE

* For 10ft by 10ft kitchen the cost will range from approximately £1500 to £9,000 plus, according to manufacturer, and at which end of range you go for. Shop around and get their brochures and price lists for precise information before you commit yourself

PURPOSE-BUILT KITCHENS

PROS

* Quality
* Purpose-built to your requirements
* Special paint and other finishes
* Personal attention from designer and manufacturer
* Lasts a lifetime

CONS

* Prices can soar if you let your enthusiasm run away with you
* Its last-a-lifetime feature may not appeal if you're planning a move in a few years

WHEN YOU'RE BUYING

* Look carefully at all manufacturers' brochures to see what they offer and to see what falls in your price range
* Make a point of visiting the showrooms of the manufacturers on your short-list. You really mustn't choose a kitchen like this from a brochure
* Take advice from your designer, make sure he knows precisely what you want, too. Together you can devise the perfect kitchen for *you*

PRICE GUIDE

* For an average 10ft by 10ft kitchen prices can start from £2000. For a large kitchen with many features expect to pay £10,000 plus

One room, three kitchens. Schreiber created these three quite difference schemes in the Halifax house to show just how dramatically the choice of colourway can affect the appearance and ambience of the room.

French polishing. Work in Corian, stainless steel, marble and granite as well as a whole range of matching furniture. Mostly they are constructed in a range of solid woods. And because they are being specially designed and built for you, all are British made – a factor that is still of great importance to many people.

One company is aware that, having spent a good deal of money on a kitchen you love, you may well wish to take it along with you when you move, so they produce a freestanding range that enables you to do just that.

You can expect the manufacturer's kitchen designer to spend some hours with you to discuss what you need in a kitchen and trying to match the design with your lifestyle and the kind of person you are. The designer wants it to be right, and will take the time to listen to all you say. After all, his reputation and that of his company is on the line every time he plans a new kitchen. But do remember it is *your* kitchen, and it is the designer's task to accommodate all your preferences – and not vice versa.

DIY DESIGN

When you are handling the whole job yourself, you will have to design and draw up the plans. This isn't difficult, but precision is the key, and there are a number of other considerations to take into account.

Position units in a way that is economical on foot slogging. Do not, for example, have the cooker on the opposite wall to the sink; or a dishwasher miles from where china and cutlery are stored. Keep refrigerator and freezer away from the hot areas, or they will work overtime to keep their low temperatures. Make sure you have provided work surfaces where you need them and that they are the correct height.

It is best to regard the original sink position as fixed unless you are able to rerun the plumbing to a new site. It is a job probably best left to an expert.

Experts call the path between the washing, cooking and storage areas 'the work triangle'. Every good working kitchen has a work triangle at its heart, even when the overall layout varies. The layout itself (single line, galley, L-shaped, or wrap-around with island site) will depend largely on personal preference and the demands made by the actual shape and size of the kitchen. Look at these layouts and see how each has its work triangle incorporated.

Good lighting is another important factor in creating a kitchen that successfully works for you. Be sure that light is positioned where you need it without forcing you to work in shadow. Don't feel that you are only able to have one central light. A strip light over your main work position can provide the chief source of illumination, but add in other strips or spotlights just where you need them – under a wall cabinet, say, so that it shines on a particular area of activity. Include a soft over-the-table light for a family diner. While the electrical work is looked at, make sure that plenty of power points are provided, and placed where you'll need them.

Whatever the shape or size of your kitchen, it is important to create a 'work triangle' between the key points of cooker, food store (usually a fridge) and sink. Keeping the sides of the triangle within a reasonable length means shorter distances to cover when preparing meals.

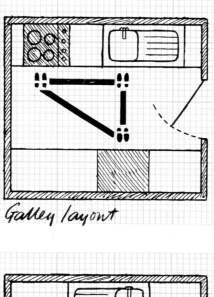

Galley layout

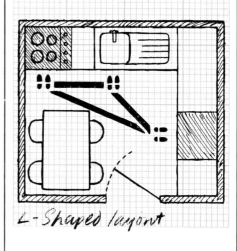

L-shaped layout

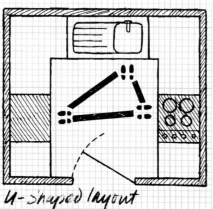

U-shaped layout

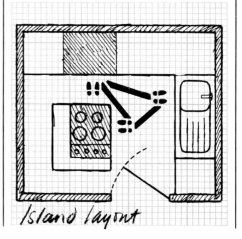

Island layout

It is surprising how spacious a comparatively small kitchen can appear if fitted with white units with pale blue trim.

MAKING PLANS

Next stage? The grand design itself. Always work to an accurate plan drawn on grid paper. It is not difficult, but it must be precise. There is nothing so frustrating than to find that a unit you particularly want doesn't quite fit.

Follow this guide to draw up your plans:

* Start by making a rough sketch of your kitchen and indicate all fixed items like doors (opening in to the room, or out), windows, radiators, boiler. Pencil in where gas pipes, plumbing and power points are located. You will then have pinpointed all the positions that are difficult to alter.

* Now measure the width, length and height of kitchen (in metres of course, or it won't transfer to a metric grid sheet) and note the measurements on your rough sketch. Add in the measurements of all the fixed items, too.

Double-check these dimensions or, better still, ask someone else to check it for you.

* Using a scale of 1:20, transfer everything to the grid sheet noting that one heavy square represents 20 centimetres of floor area.

* On a separate piece of grid paper, draw to the same scale the base area of each of the units and appliances you want to fit into the kitchen.

* Cut out the separate unit and appliance drawings, and move these around on your kitchen floorplan until you have fitted them all into a pleasing, workable arrangement. Paste them in place on the plan.

* It might be as well to photostat the plan and keep one copy safe just in case you lose the original. You don't want to have to start again from scratch!

A floorplan sketch of your existing kitchen should show the positions of all doors and windows, the existing arrangement of the key items – fridge, cooker and sink – and any existing storage. Draw in any usable adjacent space such as a utility room, and this will help you consider the prospect of making structural changes if you feel in need of more space.

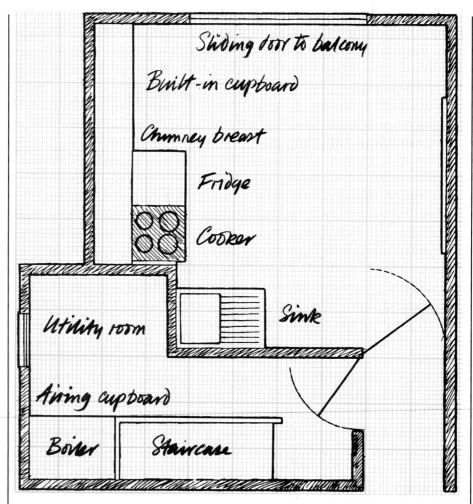

THE WORK WIZARDS

The revolution in domestic appliances over the past thirty years or so has lead us into advances never dreamed of. Indeed, the progress has been far greater in that period than in the hundreds of years that preceded it. The almost magical machines, masterminded by the ubiquitous microchip, now dominate the way we run our kitchen, if not our entire home.

Who would have thought, those years ago, that we would be cooking by microwaves or halogen light bulbs – even if we had known what they were anyway? Or that today's microchip washing machines would do everything bar fold the clothes for us?

In your new kitchen, provision will be made for modern appliances to make life easier. They can be built-in or freestanding, in a range of colours to match your scheme, or fitted with décor panels to 'hide' them within a run of matching units. These décor panels can be changed at will if you opt for a change of styling, or can even be taken with you if you move house.

The Cooker

Versatility is the name of the game. Cookers can be fuelled by gas or electricity, solid fuel, oil or liquefied petroleum gas (LPG). They can be built-in with the rest of the units in the kitchen. Or they can be split, with the oven placed quite separately from the hob. Fuels can be mixed so that you have an electric oven and grill, with a gas hob – one gas cooker uses both gas and microwaves in the oven. Even the hob itself can be mixed. There may be two gas burners, say, with two electric plates or a ceramic hob coupled with gas burners.

Ovens vary in size – from the downright too small, to a traditionally large oven capable of taking the Christmas turkey without having to force it in with the heel of your snowboot. Many British-made cookers offer two ovens, the top one of which doubles as a grill – that augurs well for the British liking for grilled food. You will notice the continental oven imports tend to have just one oven with the grill inside that. This means it is not possible to grill and bake at the same time. Also on offer from a number of manufacturers is the fan-assisted oven which circulates heat evenly, thereby cooking food at an even temperature whatever its position in the oven.

The hob is probably the part of the cooker used most and it is as well to investigate the 'cleanability' of your prospective purchase. Hobs with lots of fiddly bits to remove and keep clean may not find favour. Nor will the fascia control panels with intricate decoration – pretty and stylish when new, murder to keep clean. The most favoured hobs for cleaning must be the ceramic or

halogen types. The heating elements are sealed beneath ceramic glass and a regular wipe and polish using the special cleaners and polishes available will keep the hob looking spic and span.

A gas hob, on the other hand, with its pan supports, is less easy to keep wholesome, especially when it is necessary to dismantle the rack into several pieces for washing. There are, however, gas hobs on the market where the whole pan support will lift out in one go. Indeed, the gas cooker has undergone a design revolution in recent years – hardly recognisable from the objects our mothers used.

Refrigeration

Using the combination of a fridge with larder compartment, and a freezer, it is now possible to keep all kinds of fresh

Hiding appliances behind decor panels is the perfect way of matching them into a run of units. The oven is obvious enough, but try and spot the other appliances tucked away in this kitchen.

and other produce in exactly the right conditions to preserve it.

Fruit and vegetables can be stored in the larder or chiller compartment without becoming too cold to eat straight from the fridge. Other short-term storage can be found at a lower temperature in the main part of the refrigerator, while long-term storage takes place in the freezer – either as part of a fridge/freezer, or a separate rather larger freezer. Domestic freezers are available in enormous sizes, but don't be tempted to buy a freezer too big for your needs; apart from the unnecessarily high purchase price, it will prove more expensive to run if it is not kept full.

An ideal combination seems to be to keep a fridge/freezer in the kitchen and to store your immediate needs in the small freezer. A larger freezer can be placed in the garage or an outhouse, where the cooler ambient temperature will allow it to run more economically. Then simply restock the small freezer as necessary.

The shape of freezer you choose can depend upon the physical height of its owner. A short person will find a chest freezer painfully inconvenient to reach into for items at the bottom. But if height is not a factor, a chest freezer is the more economical type to run, since all the chill flows from an upright freezer every time you open the door. If you do buy a large chest freezer, try to organise it efficiently by colour coding packages – green labels for vegetables, say, red for meat. Keep a proper register of the items stored, with use-by dates, and cross-reference this on the labels on each package. Do use items in rotation.

A fridge can be placed in the kitchen according to the most convenient position for you. A useful trick is to raise the fridge to eye level by popping it into a built-in oven housing. Suddenly, you'll find that you can actually see that mouldering package lurking at the back and can whip it into the rubbish bin before it becomes a positive health hazard!

Washing machines

The great number of switches and buttons found on some machines these days can make the prospect of doing the laundry rather daunting. But it really doesn't take long to work out how to use the machine, and to narrow down the

Everyone's idea of the perfect country kitchen. Old ceiling beams dominate the room and make it quite unsuitable for a modern hi-tech treatment. The range of old pine kitchen units have been tailor-made and give a light, airy feel to a room despite the small windows which are in keeping with the age of the house.

It's all a question of trim: this beige kitchen and the white scheme opposite could appear bleak and uninteresting, but the application of the trimmed finishes gives both kitchens a unifying decorative theme.

facilities that are actually useful to you. Most of us will find one or two programmes that are suitable for our usual, everyday needs and stick to those. This does not mean, however, that we want to revert to the old machines. It is that we appreciate the range of choice available which gives us the facilities to use our machines exactly as we want.

It is probably best if a washing machine can be sited in a separate utility room along with a tumble drier to keep condensation away from the kitchen. This is not always possible, so aim to place the machine in a 'laundry' section of the kitchen – which sensibly needs to be near the water supply and an outlet pipe for drainage. Remember that some washing machines need a cold supply only, while others require both hot and cold.

Dishwashers

If you talk to the owner of a dishwasher you will be met with a degree of enthusiasm that may surprise you. What seems even more surprising is that so few of us have invested in these

wonderful machines. We are taking a very long time to come around to the idea – maybe we have an in-built guilt about not slaving over the sink ourselves; perhaps we think it is good discipline for our offspring to wash up for us. Indeed, people who have never had a second's worry about allowing a machine to wash their clothes suggest that owning a dishwasher is sheer, unadulterated luxury.

Banish the thought. Dishwashers are hardworking labour savers for busy households. They wash our dishes far more hygienically than we can ourselves – germs have been found to live on clean, handwashed plates simply because we are unable to use water hot enough.

Dishwashers can be built into a run of new kitchen units with a décor panel in front, if you prefer. It is sensible, though, to place it near the washing machine because it, too, needs the same plumbing and waste facility. A dishwasher will usually take a 12-place setting, but the internal fitments vary, so make sure, before you buy, that your

own china will fit. Small worktop models are available but these compact machines can really only be regarded as a practical proposition if your kitchen is large enough not to miss a vital section of worktop.

Do remember that there are certain items you should not attempt to clean in a dishwasher. Among these are wooden-handled cutlery, and fine, hand-decorated china that has not been designated 'dishwasher-proof'. Before using – indeed before *buying* – a dishwasher, do check that you will not have to restock your china and cutlery to prevent damage.

Sinks

Surely a sink is a sink is a sink, to paraphrase Shakespeare domestically. Not, we say emphatically, when it's a Work Centre. The days when the lady of the house would use a big square stone Belfast sink are but a pale memory to all but our most senior of citizens. We have run the gamut of all kinds of sink development until the newest phenomenon is the work centre, which provides all manner of combinations; two sinks, two and a half sinks (the small one's for rinsing) one and a half and a drainer. And that is to say nothing of drop-in, slot-in extras that drain and provide a chopping area for vegetables,

Knocking through the dividing wall between the kitchen and dining room can create the space for a dramatic scheme. This stunning room makes a most elegant kitchen/diner in which to entertain.

baskets for waste – easily moved for disposal – while even the mouldings are carefully engineered to direct all waste water towards the drain outlet. Many sinks come with a waste disposal unit facility which when fitted will electrically masticate most food rubbish. Only suitable waste can be pushed through the system, and this manic monster doesn't take kindly to spoons and other such items.

Taps, too, have undergone a metamorphosis. Epoxy-coated brass, stainless steel, chrome, gold plate, they come in colour co-ordinating primaries, monoblock mixers, ultra modern styling – and now, a return to the more traditional taps can be found.

When deciding on taps for your kitchen sink, do keep practical considerations at the front of your mind. A mixer with a swivelling spout is easily the most versatile arrangement, and does enable you to set the water at any temperature you want. This can make a lot of difference when it comes to tasks which mean keeping your hands under running water, such as rinsing vegetables – or cooling that scalded finger!

Extractors

Ventilating your kitchen is vital to making it a comfortable place in which to work. And maintaining a regular circulation of the air also cuts down significantly on the amount of grease and dust that inevitably accumulates on the surfaces of any kitchen.

In a modern fitted kitchen it is quite

usual to have a special extractor hood installed over the hob, and this will do an excellent job of drawing steam and grease out of the room. If you do not have, or plan to have, such a device, you should think seriously about installing a powered extractor fan.

It is important to choose a model of the right size to give the kitchen air changes at the recommended rate – namely four per hour. And to prevent draughts when the fan is not running, it should be fitted with shutters. These can be closed either automatically when the fan is switched off or by hand, by pulling a cord.

The best position in a kitchen for an extractor fan is as high up as possible, and well away from doors and windows. Close to, but not directly above, the cooker or hob is ideal. Various different models are made for fitting either through windows or through external walls. You will need to cut a hole through the wall for the latter.

Reliable and simple to operate, today's ventilator fans run surprisingly quietly and do make a dramatic difference to the freshness and cleanness – of a kitchen. And they are by no means expensive to run, using less electricity than a standard 60-watt light bulb.

There is no doubt that kitchens will continue to be the priority home improvement area for many, but the bathroom – and particularly the *second* bathroom – is fast catching up as the next room to demand attention. As you will see in the next chapter, the potential is enormous.

Another knocked-through kitchen creating an extended living space. Here, the kitchen area is contained in one part of the room, but its lack of definite boundaries aids the feeling of space overall.

BATHROOMS

For many years, the bathroom has been the 'me too' of the home improver. While the rest of the house was titivated and made beautiful, the bathroom – cold and spartan – was dealt with as an afterthought, all that has changed.

There was a time when it didn't seem to occur to homeowners that their bathrooms should be as comfortable and attractive as the rest of the house – perhaps because of the old spartan notion that the place in which daily ablutions were conducted should be purely functional, and starkly hygienic.

This attitude is changing fast. In much the same way as the kitchen has become such a focus for improvement, so the bathroom is now more and more an object of attention – particularly now that householders realise it is possible to equip to the same built-in, fitted, luxury standards as they have in their kitchens.

As such, the bathroom has become number two in the homeowner's renovation stakes, with possibly as much money spent on equipping it with new sanitaryware and accessories as was spent on the kitchen before it. Such improvements are looked on favourably for home improvement loans, which brings these luxuries within the reach of most households.

Country colours in the autumn shades of brown and soft orange bring warmth to the bathroom.

FIRST THINGS FIRST

Even before you begin to shuffle through the sanitaryware brochures, you must decide what changes you really want in your bathroom. Is it small and cramped? A change of layout could well create more space, and professional advice might help you to 'open up' the room more than you'd believe possible.

It's all a question of planning and making sure that you are building in all you require. In even the tiniest of bathrooms, storage cupboards can be built over or built under; minute spaces can be kitted out for keeping towels or for spare loo rolls. More space may be gained by fitting a corner bath; or why have a bath at all? If you like showers and can forego the luxury of a good long soak in the bath, you might as well fit a shower only, and open up the rest of the bathroom for all other kinds of luxury.

If the space factor is *really* critical, consider knocking down the wall between bathroom and separate wc – making sure you get professional advice if it is load-bearing. Or you may have an unused spare bedroom that can be converted into a bathroom. Indeed, if you are swopping bathroom and bedroom, your tiny bathroom can still be put to good use by converting it into a small bedroom with bunk beds, or study/office. If this seems a viable idea, do try to use a room that is close to the house's soil and waste pipes. It's not impossible to reroute plumbing or to put in a new soil pipe, but it is far less complicated if you don't have to do so.

Only tackle such work yourself if you are a competent handyperson. Leaky joints or an incorrectly angled waste pipe are more hassle than they're worth. See page 107 for plumbing details.

Treat the bathroom like the kitchen. Fitted kitchen manufacturers have now moved into the fitted bathroom business – to great effect. This country-cottage-style scheme has been hand painted, and fitted out with plenty of storage space.

FITTED BATHROOMS

A new and definite vogue is for fitting
out bathrooms as fully as any kitchen
might be, with vanity units, cupboards
and cabinets. Indeed, in many cases, it is
kitchen manufacturers who have
contributed to the trend, which really
does put the bathroom into a whole new
category – a room with every
convenience, and in which you are
pleased to spend time. Both modern and
traditional looks can be achieved with
ranges of units in laminates or in
mahogany, pine and oak.

With so much space available in a
range of cupboard units, pressure can be
eased on storage requirements in the
bedroom. And since many women put
on their make-up in the bathroom
anyway, it may be sensible to fit it out
with a dressing table. The large
bathroom can therefore not only be
enjoyable as such, but can have the
merit of additional functions. The small
bathroom can be successfully fitted out,
too – and manufacturers offer units
specially suited to smaller spaces.

THE OPTIONS

The choice of bathroom equipment
encompasses a host of shapes, sizes and
colours, with styles that range from the
quaintly Victorian (sometimes made
from original mouldings) through to the
frankly futuristic.

Washbasins

Basins can be wall-hung, inset into a
vanity unit or pedestal standing.
Pedestals usually stand at a height of
815mm (32 in), but if this is a little high
or low for you, consider a wall-hung
model that can be fixed at any height you
choose. Decide upon the size you need
as they can vary between the tiny
hand-rinse version for cloakrooms, to a
really large basin big enough to bath the
baby in! Shapes vary greatly, too –
between oval, round, square and even
corner versions.

Baths

Acrylic, glass-fibre, cast-iron or pressed
steel coated with porcelain enamel are
the materials offered to you, and these
can come in a large variety of shapes and
finishes: look out for colours, two-tone,
metallic or marbled surfaces. Watch

Stunning. There can be no other
word for it. The raised platform
gives the room its exciting sense
of shape, with the sunken bath as
centrepiece. The decorative
drama of the scheme is further
emphasised by yellow and blue
accent colours.

Victorian styles are very much in vogue. All kinds of sanitaryware and accessories, in a range of colours and design, are available. Traditional looks are combined with the latest high-quality materials to provide luxurious, easy-care and practical baths, basins and WCs – the best of both worlds.

out, too, for the pretty floral designs on Victorian-styled sanitaryware. Shapes offered include corner, round, oval, clover leaf, and the regular rectangular. Moulded armrests, soap trays, seats and backs can be found. Many baths now include a whirlpool system – at a price. Bathing has become a whole new experience since the advent of the whirlpool (or Jacuzzi) where the water turns and tumbles and pulsates, providing a most stimulating and – we are told – health-giving bath. There is even a shower on the market that offers what can only be described as an 'all over' massage. Designed specially for tiny bathrooms, there is the small, deep soaking tub that can be fitted in where most baths cannot.

Lavatories

It's hard to imagine a lavatory that can be called 'stylish' but that is just what they are intended to be these days! Slimline, designer models that cause not a twinge of shame. Neat and petite cisterns are usually low level – unless a high-level, Victorian-style cistern is installed with brass fittings and a pull chain. Some models have a concealed cistern which leaves only the flush handle on show, but make sure you have ready access to the cistern.

Bidets

From a time when, not so long ago, the British first came upon the French bidet and thought it was a footbath, we now know that it is for a rather more 'intimate' purpose. What's more, they are now quite commonly fitted in the British bathroom.

Water enters the bidet in various ways: either over the rim, through the taps, or around the rim heating the edge of it at the same time. Some bidets also have an ascending douche spray fitted into the base, though check these out, since they can give some trouble in operating. Bidets are fitted facing the wall, so when positioning it take care that you are allowing enough knee room for all the possible users. Get the person with the longest legs to sit on it before the final fixing takes place, just to make sure.

Showers

You have the choice of a shower with tray for standing in, with drainage through the waste system, or you can have a tiled floor sloping towards the drain outlet which dispenses with the need for a tray. It all depends what kind of flooring you want. If a tiled floor is the method you go for you'll have to be specially careful with the grouting, and

The shower door as an art form. This one has the extra merit of being inward-opening, and thus valuably space-saving.

that the tiles are waterproof. For further information on showers (see page 112).

COLOUR CONCEPTS

Wild sage, cameo pink, damask, sorrento blue, bali brown. The colour names sound like lyrics from a love song and quite belie the down-to-earth purpose for which they are designed. While it may not be wise to go off on wild flights of fancy with your colour schemes since the sanitaryware colour will dominate, careful selection of toning colours can produce a pleasing – and dramatic – overall effect. A rich maroon, for example, will be stunning teamed with grey, navy or soft beige. A glowing sunshine gold will be enhanced by warm sienna and browns. If the colour of the equipment is kept low key, the scheme to go with it can be infinitely more varied. Indeed, a white suite can form the basis of a softly feminine scheme, or a stark monochromatic look with contrasting black tiles and white carpet.

MAKING PLANS

Once you have chosen the sanitaryware, you can set about planning the bathroom to its best advantage. Draw up an accurate floorplan of the room on graph paper. Mark on the plan all the immovable objects like the window, door, radiator. Note whether the door swings in, or out, since that will affect the amount of space available. If it is taking up too much room by swinging

Rich rose pink brings style and warmth to this traditionally decorated bathroom.

into the room, it is worth seeing if you can hang the door in reverse so that it opens outwards. Take care that an out-swinging door doesn't cause problems by being placed at the top of a stairway, or in a narrow passage. Otherwise, consider a sliding door, either on the bathroom or landing side of the wall.

Cut out accurate to-scale pieces to represent the bathroom fixtures, and juggle these around the floor plan in various positions until satisfied with your plan. To avoid the need to alter the position of an existing soil pipe, you should locate the new wc as close as possible to the site of the old one. Remember, too, that bath and basin wastes should be within reasonable reach of existing drainage outlets.

PLUMBING IN

If you cannot contemplate handling the plumbing yourself, call in the professionals. But if you're reasonably adept at most DIY chores, plumbing shouldn't present any particular difficulties, especially if aided by a good reference book. This brief outline on fitting a new bath and basin will help you decide whether you might be able to tackle it yourself or will need professional aid:

* Cut off water supply and turn on taps to drain water until they run dry. There may be stop valves fitted to the water outlets close to the bath. If so, turn those off so that you don't have to drain the storage tank too.

* Make sure both central heating and/or immersion heater are switched off.
* Disconnect taps by undoing the nut linking the supply pipe to tap tail.
* Disconnect waste pipes from basin and bath outlets; buckets and cloths to the ready in case some water is spilled.
* Remove bath and basin. Take them straight out of the house to give you working space.
* Cover lavatory to prevent building rubble blocking the system.
* Strip off wallcoverings and/or tiles. Make good surfaces.
* Check the floor under the bath to make sure that seeping water hasn't rotted the boards. Replace if necessary.

* While access is still easy, fit new taps, combined overflow and waste outlets. If new fittings are to be positioned in the same place as the old, you will need only the special seating washers supplied with most taps and waste outlets. If position is to change, you'll need to alter the existing plumbing – either by extending or shortening the pipework.
* Position new bath and basin according to manufacturer's instructions. Attach old tap connectors with fibre washers to new tap tails. Use PTFE tape wrapped round tap tail for watertight seal.

If that doesn't sound too daunting, it's worth buying the appropriate reference books, or borrowing them from the library and tackling it yourself.

Sanitaryware in stark black works well within this imaginative and boldly dramatic decorative scheme.

SECOND THOUGHTS

It may be that the bathroom you have is just fine as a family room, but you would like a second, *en suite*, bathroom for your own personal use. It would be ideal if you have a small box room next to your bedroom which can be converted to a bathroom with access knocked through to your room. If you wish, you can block off the old exit, so that the bathroom truly becomes personal to you.

If the necessary space for a second bathroom is not available, consider placing a wash basin or even a shower cabinet in your room. Where there is space, it might be possible to install a shower cabinet outside your room on a landing.

The aim should be to provide comfort and convenience to everyone living in the house and to those who occasionally visit. So, if funds permit, it is only right that extra washing and lavatory facilities are on offer.

FINISHING TOUCHES

With the sanitaryware installed, there is more to do if the bathroom is to have the mark of your own taste and personality. Your choice of décor and accessories gives the room the touch of individuality that will make it special. So ask yourself these questions:

* What style of bathroom do you want – modern or traditional?
* Do you want it to be warm and welcoming?
* Do you prefer the cool hi-tech look?
* Do you like the bright primary colours, or the soft shades that co-ordinate with the suite's colour?

Then look at the accessories available and build up the look you want.

* For a traditional room, seek out Victorian-style pillar taps, pretty fluted lightshades and fittings, mahogany-framed mirrors, old

The 'Dolphin' suite, a revival of a design that first appeared in the 1880s, looks as good as ever, even in a bathroom decorated in today's style.

prints, plants galore, frilly curtains, or Austrian blinds.

* Go modern with bright colours, futuristic tap fittings, tiles, chrome and glass. Bold splashes of colour can be introduced with piles of fluffy towels and a blind at the window.
* Accent colours can be additionally picked out with small guest soaps displayed attractively in a large brandy glass; or with shelves and soapdishes, bath oils, powder puffs – even the toothbrushes.
* Manufacturers of bathroom accessories such as vanity units and soap trays now market items in exactly the same colours as those used by the major sanitaryware producers. This, sadly, is as far as it goes, for there no longer seems to be colour standardisation among sanitaryware manufacturers, who prefer to produce their bathroom suites in their own exclusive colour ranges. This makes it virtually impossible to mix and match items from different manufacturers.

BATH SAFELY

* Don't forget that water and electricity make a very dangerous combination.
* Lighting in the bathroom should only be operated by a pull cord, or from outside the room. Light fittings must not be close to the shower or in a position above the basin where it would be all too easy to touch both light and wet tap at the same time.
* Only use an electric fire if it is a wall fixed model operated by a pull cord. Never prop an electric fire or appliance on or near the bath while bathing. It's a quick way to an early grave.
* Baths and shower trays can be very slippery underfoot. Look out for non-slip surfaces, or use a rubber safety mat to stand on.
* For the elderly or handicapped, choose a bath with moulded grab handles. Some have built-in seats or pulleys to help the infirm in and out.

Handsome and luxurious, this mahogany-framed bath has a timeless stylishness that will last and last.

SHOWERS

All things to all people, showers can give us a brisk, refreshing start to the day, or the softly sensuous sensation of being gently doused with a warm enveloping spray. For either of these highly desirable effects, the price could not be more reasonable, as it only costs around 3p for a good five minutes' worth of showering. A shower uses a mere fifth of the hot water required for a bath, so to its list of merits add economy. Installing a traditional mixer shower will be a problem if there is not enough 'head' between the base of the cold water tank and the shower outlet. Without at least a metre of distance between the two, the

pressure will be inadequate to give a satisfactory flow of water. One solution is to raise the tank to a higher position in your roof space. Another, less complicated answer is to boost the flow with a shower pump. Alternatively, go for an instantaneous electric shower instead.

Water supply

The 'indirect' system is the most common type of domestic plumbing. This is where a cold water storage tank in the loft feeds the separate hot water tank below it. With this system you can opt for a bath/shower mixer which simply replaces the bath taps. Or a shower cabinet with its own hot and cold water plumbing. You can also choose an instantaneous electric shower connected to the mains; this has the advantage of heating only just as much water as you need at any one time.

The 'direct' system of plumbing means that the cold taps all over the house are fed directly from the mains so that a plumbed-in shower would be a mixture of high pressure cold water and low pressure hot water – contrary to water bylaws. In this case the instantaneous electric shower is the only type you can install.

The options

Quite the simplest form of shower is the bath/shower mixer that replaces the bath taps. The existing bath acts as a shower tray, and as long as the surround is adequately tiled and grouted, and a shower curtain fitted (remember to tuck the curtain into the bath when showering), that is really all you need. A mixer shower head, separate from the bath's plumbing, can also be placed over the bath.

Mixer showers

Can be fitted with a shower head on a flexible hose that can be raised or lowered as required. On the other hand, a fully plumbed-in shower leaves only the shower head visible and its control panel. With this, you must be able to adjust the angle of the shower head easily as you're certainly not going to be able to alter the height. Position the head on the side wall of the enclosure so the spray doesn't jet through the doorway when the door is opened.

Electric showers heat the cold-water supply instantaneously to provide a thermostatically controlled hot spray – at a modest cost.

The shower equivalent of a 'whirlpool' bath: separate jets, in addition to the overhead nozzle, provide body-massaging sprays.

Instantaneous showers

Run either on gas or electricity, these showers have the advantage of heating only the required amount of cold mains water – almost instantly. They are easy to install, with all the important parts of the shower fitted into its control box. The flow rate will vary slightly according to the temperature of the water. A winter shower, therefore, where icy water is being heated, will deliver less flow because it takes longer to heat up the water. With showers of a larger heating capacity of 8kw and over, this effect is minimised. The instantaneous shower offers adaptability since it requires only a cold supply, which allows you to place it almost anywhere within reasonable access of a drainage outlet.

Accessories

You will have to protect the area surrounding your shower from splashing – or worse. A shower over the bath will need only a shower curtain, or a single glass or acrylic panel, and adequate tiling on the walls. If you are placing a shower elsewhere a proper enclosure will be necessary. The most popular kind is a shower cabinet. You can make up these yourself, or they are sold by a number of manufacturers ready assembled. They can have sliding doors (to save space), swing-open doors, with two walls suitable for a corner position, or full four-walled cabinets that can be sited just where you want them. They are offered in a range of colours and designs, but do check that they are of shatterproof acrylic, or safety glass.

Shower trays, too, are produced in a variety of shapes, sizes and depths. Some have a finished edge, others don't since they are designed to be sunk into a tiled floor. Choose from ceramic, acrylic or cast iron in a range of colours to match the rest of your sanitaryware – the colour choice is huge.

If you hate the idea of a shower cubicle – do without. A shower curtain can protect from splashes, or a shoulder-high, tiled partition wall will offer privacy, without feeling shut in. The partition wall – or even a more substantial tiled cubicle – is easy to construct with timber, stud and plasterboard, and then tiled to your choice.

This pretty en suite, installed at the Halifax House, has a neat vanity unit and shelf system providing valuable storage space.

You don't have to opt for a shower tray either if you'd prefer to go for a fully-tiled floor sloping towards the drain outlet – remember the shower in your continental holiday hotel? Take care, though, that the tiles are suitable for a regular dousing, and that the grouting is good and waterproof. Watch out for signs of cracked or chipped grouting, and replace quickly before water is allowed to seep through and under, causing all kinds of damage below.

Installation

Safety and efficiency are the criteria applied to fitting a shower. For it to work well and be safe to use, it must be installed properly. Take your plumber's advice about the type of shower most suited to your needs if there is any doubt about the space between tank and shower head being adequate.

If you are a competent DIY enthusiast, there is really no reason why

The built-in look: luxury bathrooms now rival fitted kitchens for smart coordinated looks and copious space for storage.

A corner bath looks special and saves space – giving a sense of style and roominess.

you cannot carry out the fairly simple job of installing a mixer shower yourself, as long as you follow the instructions with care.

Installing an instantaneous shower is an easy job, too, but because of the electric work, it must be done in accordance with the Institution of Electrical Engineers' regulations. It isn't worth the risk of dicing daily with a faulty electrical connection. Call in a qualified electrician to do this part of the work for you, or at least check it out. A gas powered instantaneous shower should also have the installation carried out by the experts. Check with your gas board for a CORGI registered member in your area.

Right sites

The advent of the instantaneous shower and the shower cubicle means that there is nowhere around the house that's impractical for siting it. If you have a large family you could, if you were inclined, provide a shower cubicle for every one of them in all kinds of unlikely locations about the house. Or are they such unlikely sites? An outside privvy would make a great conversion, so too

SHOWER SAFELY

* For complete safety, use a thermostatically controlled shower which automatically maintains your chosen temperature and flow rate, even if someone turns on a tap in another room, or a loo is flushed. Instantaneous showers will also offer a stable temperature. A manual shower where you adjust the flow and temperature yourself is less expensive, but you can run the risk of scalding – or being doused with ice cold water – when water is being used in other parts of the house.
* Make sure, too, that the shower has a non-slip surface or rubber safety mat; and for the elderly, good grab handles and a seat.
* Never use standard glass for a shower surround if you are making up one yourself. Choose specially toughened safety glass or extra thick 6mm-8mm glass approved to British Standard 6202. Safety plastic should also be used for synthetic screens. While 'missiles' do not commonly hurtle about the average household it could prevent serious injuries if someone should stumble and push a limb through a shower cabinet.

ELECTRIC SHOWERS

MAKE	MODEL	POWER	WATER PRESSURE
Aquatron	Rio	7kW	15-150 psi
	Sigma	7kW	15-150 psi
	Sigma	8kW	15-150 psi
	Viva 7/8	4 & 7/8kW	15-150 psi
Dolphin	840	8.4kW	15-150 psi
Heatrae Sadia	Accolade	7 or 8kW	14.5-150 psi
	Carousel	7 or 8kW	14.5-150 psi
	Showerplan	7 or 8kW	14.5-150 psi
	Touchflow	7 or 8kW	14.5-150 psi
Mira	Miralex ts-2	7kW	13-145 psi
	Supreme	4 or 7kW	10-145 psi
	Supreme 8.3	4.9 or 8.3kW	12-150 psi
Triton	T100E	7.2 or 8.4kW	12-150 psi
	T80	7 or 8kW	12-100 psi
	T70	7 or 8kW	12-100 psi
	T60	7kW	12-100 psi

psi = lbs per square inch mains water pressure
All these electric showers are fitted with a thermal cut out

Manufacturers of thermostatic showers which take your existing hot and cold supply and control the temperature you set are:
The Finnish Valve Co's Windsor range;
Meynell Showers Ltd's Elegance collection;
Grohe's Relaxa showers; Aqualisa's range of fittings and Walker Crosweller's Mira showers.

would an old larder. What about that spare space under the stairs? How about a shower tucked into a corner in the utility room? Upstairs in the bedroom making it luxuriously *en suite*. On the landing itself, to ease pressure on the bathroom? In a loft conversion, or down in the cellar. All can offer the small amount of floor space needed for increasing your facilities.

What is more, the overall cost of making such installations need not be high. It's certainly cheaper to put in two – even three – showers than to install a complete extra bathroom.

BEDROOMS

More than any other room in the house, the bedroom gives us our own private space, our sanctuary from the wear and tear of day-to-day life. All the more reason to make it individual, and very specifically tailored to our needs

Put a bed in a bare room and, for all practical purposes, you have a bedroom. Add a few pieces of furniture; apply the veneer of wallcoverings, paint, carpets and curtains; give it a little extra with well-chosen accessories and, before you know it, you have created a room in which it is good to luxuriate, and which projects that special individuality so important when furnishing a home.

As in the other rooms of the house, you can impose a style, an ambience, by your choice of décor. Take three totally different sorts of people, for example:

City slickers look tailored – almost hi-tech – for them, none of the frilly frippery. Bright colours, contrasting with stark black or white. Purely functional furniture, with flush-faced wardrobe fitments incorporating a neat dressing table and drawer space. Curtains will be utterly simple or even dispensed with altogether in favour of Venetian blinds. The floor may be covered with plain, bold, polished tiles, or painted wooden boards, left bare. The bed linen will echo the slick modern feel in bright primaries.

Cottage dwellers – not that you have to live in a cottage to achieve this look! Here come the frills, but not the over-elaborate flounces of Austrian blinds. Curtains and bed linen alike will be pretty florals edged with frilled borders. Pine furniture – new or Victorian

Simply elegant: a cool, uncluttered bedroom in the city-slicker style. In a scheme that is predominantly grey and white, the stark splashes of accent colour give interest and a sense of dimension to the room.

stripped – will abound. Or perhaps it will be painted in pastels with a home-spun dragged effect. A simple washstand with Victorian washbowl and jug. Pretty flowered wallpaper either matching or contrasting with the fabrics. Country greens, browns and pinks dominate the scheme.

Truly traditional – mahogany, or one of the other rich dark woods look good here. Three-mirrored dressing table with elegant little drawers. Freestanding wardrobe and a chest of drawers form part of a suite and sturdy head and footboards to the bed. Regency stripes or simple cool designs for the walls. Contrasting fabric for the curtains with matching quilted bedcover.

Any of these styles are easy to put together and many more besides – for inspiration, browse through magazines and catalogues, or your favourite department stores. Then plan out the room before you buy a thing.

Here's another thing to think out. For what purpose are you going to use the

A bold colour for the walls of a large room such as this lavish, two-level scheme gives a warmer, more intimate effect – and all the more so if the ceiling and floor are treated in lighter tones.

Pine furniture, a pretty floral border around doorway and dado rail and accessories with a nostalgic theme all contribute to a country-cottage effect for the bedroom.

Bedroom furniture can be decorative as well as practical – as witnessed by this handsome cupboard in the linen-press style. The linen chest at the foot of the bed, plus the smart, comfortable armchair, bring an extra dimension to the room.

bedroom. Let's face it, bedrooms are used in any number of ways besides sleeping; indeed, what a pity to have a truly special room if you only see it for the few minutes before you sleep, and during the mad rush while you get ready for work in the mornings.

Many people like to use their bedrooms as a quiet study area or work room away from the family. In this case, a work table or desk needs to be installed; or maybe a drawing board is needed; or a sewing machine.

If you need a bolt-hole in which to escape, consider installing a small TV set in your bedroom, with a couple of comfortable armchairs and the means of

making yourself a drink or a snack – an electric kettle or coffee maker, or if you're out to make it extra special, put in a microwave oven and a tiny fridge.

ROOM FOR A CHILD – OR TWO

A child's room should wear well, be easy to clean, and be safe both to play and to sleep in. And it should have furniture that stands up to the rough treatment meted out by youngsters.

So go for washable wallcoverings or paint (lead-free of course). Choose sturdy furniture that is not going to tip on top of a child impatiently trying to pull open a drawer. Make sure that unused electric sockets have childproof covers. If buying furniture specially, try to make sure that it 'grows' with the child and will still be usable for a teenager.

Make sure plenty of storage space is provided, and see that it is at heights that a child can reach – balancing on a chair to open a wall cupboard can be dangerous.

All kinds of fun characters are depicted on wallcoverings and fabrics, but do remember before you spend a fortune fixing the room for a would-be train driver – boy or girl! – that one craze can soon be supplanted by another, with accompanying demands for redecoration. Plain walls, plus lots of removable posters, friezes and the like may well make more sense.

If you're carpeting the room, choose something that is inexpensive and easy to keep clean such as one of the acrylic mixtures. Or you will find that vinyl can be a good alternative to carpet, especially the cushioned vinyl which is soft and warm to the touch and easy to clean, too. But do not put rugs on the floor, as these can easily trip up playing children.

Purpose-designed for the needs of a child, this cheerful scheme fits a bunk bed and all storage units into one end of the room – leaving generous floor space for playing.

More good use of space: these ingeniously designed units form a compact and exciting bedroom scheme for a school-age child.

Take care what form of heating you use in a child's room. Radiators are probably the safest to use in this area where safety is of special importance. If you use an electric fire to boost the warmth in very cold weather, it's preferable to use a wall heater as this should dispense with the need for trailing wires and doesn't allow the child to place anything flammable nearby. It is not wise to have a gas or coal fire in a child's room.

Have you ever wished that you could be a child again so that you, too, could have one of those ingenious bunk beds-cum-desk-cum-dressing table-cum-cupboard – but, of course, with a stepladder? Bedroom furniture for children is such *fun* these days. Where space is short, remember that some beds fold away into the wall to make more playing room.

GOING SPARE

If your spare room has sufficient space, it's as well to furnish it with twin beds against the possibility that you will be catering for a couple. Alternatively, an armchair that converts to a single bed will provide the second bed when

necessary. It is pleasant, too, if you can provide an extra wash basin or vanity unit which will ease pressure on the bathroom when you have visitors.

As the spare bedroom is often just that – only used occasionally – some people like to use the space for other purposes, too. This is when it can be kitted out as a work room or study, but try to use furniture with a double purpose – the desk that easily becomes a dressing table, the bed that can have a tumble of cushions to provide a sofa – and make sure that you have enough storage space to be able to tuck away all your paraphernalia when visitors arrive. Without this facility, your visiting friends and family will feel less than welcome if they are tucked into a corner of a room obviously used for other, more important purposes.

SLEEPING PARTNERS

To a comfortable bed that properly supports your back, add quality bedding and you have a recipe for a compatible relationship. First, in the natural progression of things, you should 'think bed'. And that means realising that buying one is more than choosing a mattress with a pretty cover.

To start with, if you have been sleeping in your bed for more than ten years it could be near the end of its natural life span. And after 15 years of continuous use you should be replacing it. To expect a bed to last beyond its time will give you a whole heap of trouble – both in terms of the quality of your sleep, and because trying to sleep on the bumps and dips of a worn-out mattress causes all kinds of stress on your body.

When buying, it's vitally important to test out the bed – yes, right there in the store. Lie on it, stretching full length as if you were in your own bed at home. And if it's a double bed, make sure that your partner tests it along with you. This is not a time for coyness!

Although we vary in our liking for soft or hard mattresses, it is vital that our spines are kept in correct alignment. It makes sense that heavier people need a firmer bed otherwise it is very difficult for the spine to be held correctly. When testing the bed, see if you can feel the mattress pushing back against your body – this is the degree of firmness you should aim for.

A practical and very attractive feature for a guest room, a traditionally styled, but fully plumbed-in, washstand makes visitors feel particularly welcome.

For a good night's sleep you need enough room, so don't buy a bed that is too small – and that means length as well as width. The standard double is 150cm, and the length for both sizes runs to 200cm. for those that need larger beds because of their height or girth, 'specials' can be made, and are well worth the extra cost. Elderly people prefer a bed that is high enough for them to be able to get in and out without difficulty.

The most common type of mattress is open sprung (metal coils in a padded cover). Where the springs are all in one piece it is known as continuous springing. The most expensive springing, pocket springing, separates individual springs in fabric pockets so that each will perform independently. In sprung mattresses of this kind, the strength of the springs determine the firmness of the bed, though this can be moderated by the amount of padding packed beneath the cover. With a foam mattress, on the other hand, it is simply the density of the foam that varies its firmness.

One word of warning. If your fancy runs to a pine bed with a slatted wooden base, you will find that this makes a hard mattress even harder. Go for a rather softer mattress to compensate, and don't be tempted to buy one with pocket springing. This type of spring tends to rub away on the slatted base and, despite its extra cost, will wear out much too quickly.

SLEEP TIGHT

Buying the bed, not surprisingly, is only half the story. The bedding, too, will have some bearing on whether your nights are good ones or not.

The advent of easy-care bed linens – like polyester/cotton – has revolutionised the laundry side of things. Just imagine what it must have been like to wash by hand, hang out to dry, laboriously iron, then a spell in the airing cupboard before putting back on the bed. Now it's possible to strip the bed, wash the sheets, dry and have them back on the bed before you've rubbed the sleep out of your eyes!

This does mean that you no longer need a huge supply of bed linen to carry you through laundering. On the other hand, designs, too, have been

revolutionised, enabling us to change the moods and appearance of the bedroom at a whim; and the temptation these days is still to have a good supply of linen in order to take advantage of the variety of designs and colours on offer. How easy it is to change from pretty florals in spring or autumn tones, to bold geometrics in bright primaries or dark paisley tones; from frills to plain no-nonsense styles. This way, it's possible to use the bed linen that either suits your mood, or suits the season – the warm, cosy designs will seem to take the

Room at the top: a reasonably spacious loft can be converted to make a comfortable and airy master bedroom.

The cool looks of white furniture will not make a bedroom look uncomfortably cold if the overall scheme incorporates warm colours on floor and walls.

chill out of the air when the temperature outside drops below zero, yet that same design will make you swelter when the heat of the summer really arrives, as it sometimes does!

Some manufacturers market 'bedroom related' products that match their bed linen. Little cushions, lampshades, small jug and bowl sets, plant pots and so on. The ranges are large and still growing, so visit the chain stores and specialist shops to get a feel for what is available.

All the pretty designs in the world will not give you a good night's sleep if the fabrics they come in are not to your liking. Taste in bed linen is a very personal thing; some people simply won't sleep between anything other than crisp starched cotton (so back to the laundry here), while others, though liking the cotton-like feel of polyester/cotton, can't stand the texture of nylon against their skins, or the warm, clinging feel of the flocked nylon that was so popular at one time. Some of us don't feel 'right' unless the bed clothes weigh quite heavily on us, others like warmth, but want their bedding to be as light as a whisper. It's as well to be aware of all these things before making any purchases – there's nothing so useless as a pair of sheets that *no-one* likes sleeping between!

TO QUILT OR NOT TO QUILT

While the number of us converted to the continental quilt is considerable and growing all the time (I suspect that their popularity is greatest among the bed *makers*) there remains a sizeable number of old-school devotees to the blanket. These are much heavier than the quilt (or duvet), which obviously will be popular with the 'heavy bed' faction. In the depth of winter, as many as four blankets may be needed, but they can at least be peeled off according to the ambient temperature of the room. Wool blankets can be bad news for allergy sufferers, so look for the synthetic fibre blankets if there is an allergy problem in your household.

The duvet, on the other hand, is extremely light and very warm. It is channelled and then filled with a bulky material in order to keep the filling well distributed. It completely surrounds the body so that natural heat is retained in a

The luxury of space: more than just a bedroom, this elegant and comfortable scheme doubles as a private sitting room. The two functions of the room are unified by common theme of wickerwork furnishings.

Minimally furnished, this bedroom shows true creative flair not just for its oriental-style absence of clutter but for its economy; besides the chair, every item was picked up second hand from junk shops.

type of cocoon. The cost of a duvet is determined by the quality of the filling and the amount used. The warmth it provides also depends on these factors. So that you can choose a duvet of the appropriate warmth, the tog rating system has been devised. Each duvet is thus classified, and you can easily select the type that is most suited to your requirements. See the tog rating chart below.

HOW WARM?

The warmth of a duvet is measured in togs. This peculiar word is simply the measure of the rate at which body heat escapes through the covering of your duvet. The higher the tog – the less heat gets out.

The British Standards Institution has recently approved a new tog rating system. It ranges from a 4.5 minimum tog-rating duvet – a lightweight version suitable for summer use – through to a rating of 13.5 minimum – the warmest of all.

Warmth Classifications

4.5	6.0	7.5	9.0	10.5	12.0	13.5
tog	tog	tog	tog	tog	tog	tog
min	min	min	min	min	min	min
SUMMER USE		WARM			EX WARM	

Simply choose the tog rating which is most suitable for you.

WHAT FILLINGS?

Man-made fillings are the most reasonably priced. They are washable and non-allergenic. These are likely to be the least warm, though not always. Check the tog rating before buying. *Natural fillings* are warm and cosy and will snuggle round you in a way that the man-made fillings won't. Goose or duck down gives the warmest and lightest filling, but it is more expensive too. Down and feather fillings (more down, less feather) or feather and down (much more feather, less down) are also popular and less expensive.

Always use a cover on your duvet to protect it from dirt and dust. They're also much more suited to frequent washing. The duvet itself can be cleaned occasionally. If it is made from a man-made filling, it can be machine washed, but follow the instructions carefully. It is possible to wash duvets with natural fillings – with care – but it is far better that they are cleaned professionally. Most dry cleaners offer a duvet cleaning service. And when you buy, check that it carries the British Standard number 5335.

Other ways of keeping warm in bed are provided by electric blankets and under blankets (which look more like a sheepskin rug). The under blanket provides a soft warm base on which to sleep and as this is beneath the body, it seems to warm up the bed more quickly than usual. The electric blanket has now been improved to such a degree that you can sleep with it switched on – even the underblanket models – and they can be laundered in a washing machine. Dual heat models are available for sleeping partners who have different heat requirements.

ON BUYING

Good fit is the main criterion when buying bed linens – especially when purchasing fitted sheets. Before shopping, take measurements of bed and pillows. It is better that linen is too big than too small. If an over-large mattress is stuffed into a too-small fitted sheet, the stress and strain on the seams will be considerable. If you are buying a bedcover, measure the bed made-up so you don't mistakenly choose one that hangs short at the sides and foot. To measure up for a valance to cover the bed base, take the measurement from the floor to the top of the base and then make sure that this is the same depth as the frill of the valance. If you are buying a valanced sheet which is an undersheet with valance attached, measure from the top of the mattress to the floor, and then make sure that the total measurement of the frill plus side of sheet is the same.

For unfitted sheets, make sure that there is a generous tuck-in allowance. There is nothing more miserable than for the bedcovers to become untucked in the middle of the night. The same, of course, goes for blankets; duvets, too, since they seem to be the rogues of the bed chamber in their unfailing capacity to slide off the bed when covering a restless sleeper. A larger than required duvet seems to be the answer, so that if you can run to king size on a double sized bed, or double on a single bed the problem should solve itself.

PILLOW TALK

Whether you like hard or soft pillows, one or two, the aim should be to give your head and neck adequate support. Test a pillow by plumping it up and then laying it across your hand. If it droops across your hand, it's time to replace it. Try to go for a quality pillow – though you might be shaken to find that you can

A stylish answer to the need for combining studying and sleeping spaces. A smart desk in the style of other bedroom furnishings fits well into the overall scheme.

pay as much as £45 for one at the top of the range. You'll find the better quality foam pillows will give you good service, as will pillows with Terylene Superloft and Dacron Hollofil. Blends of curled poultry and duck feathers give a fairly springy pillow, or for good support try pure duck feathers.

To care for your pillows, give them a shake every day and air them regularly. Foam pillows can be sponged clean in warm soapy water every few months. But rinse well, and remove excess water with an absorbent towel. Dry off in the airing cupboard. Pillows made from a washable fibre can be cleaned a couple of times a year. Follow the makers' instructions, though. If your pillows have a natural down or feather filling, send them to a professional cleaner every two or three years.

Good ideas for a small bedroom: fresh and sunny colours heighten the sense of space, and the interesting shutters give emphasis to the window, thus boosting the feeling of light in the room.

LIVING ROOMS

Before you choose a paint colour or wallpaper pattern, a complete living-room plan must be formulated. Furnishing arrangements, lighting, wiring and other vital aspects of the room need consideration well in advance of final decisions on how to decorate

The very first decision must be whether or not you are going to refurnish completely – and there can be few of us who would wish to, or could afford to.

Unless your existing furniture is really only fit for the local 'amenity site' or you are planning a total change of style, you are likely to have at least a couple of pieces that will enhance your new scheme. Indeed, it may be those very pieces that remain that add the individual character to a room otherwise newly furnished throughout.

You don't, of course, have to buy new if you are replacing furniture. Antiques can be very costly, but much good second-hand furniture needn't be. The search for an excellent piece at a bargain price is as exhilarating as owning it. And if you are prepared to carry out some restoration work yourself, it should be that much easier to find furniture within your budget. Try the auctions, but be wary of the dealers who are also bidding for good items to resell in their shops.

You will sometimes find out-of-town villages that have a name for antiques – simply because antique dealers seem to like to trade in an area known for it. So once a couple of shops have opened in an area, more come along to join them until you can spend an enjoyable day roaming around from shop to shop – each one possibly specialising in items just a little bit different in period, or price, from its neighbour.

But don't head in the direction of antiques without reliable advice. A knowledgeable friend may give you confidence, but do read up on the subject first. There are a number of books available giving valuable assistance to beginners. Look out in particular for *Miller's Guide to Antiques*.

Increasingly there is a market these days for junk shop furniture. Indeed, the fun of the search can be just as intense as for the more serious antique buyers. You need a good eye for possibilities in old run-down furniture. Imagine what it would look like with its peeling paint or varnish removed, with a smart new surface applied, with its knobs or handles replaced.

Do make sure you have a home for any item of furniture that catches your eye. If it is really too big and clumsy to fit well in your home, it will hardly seem the bargain you first thought it. Make sure, too, that its structure is basically sound; that it doesn't have telltale signs of woodworm (although you can treat woodworm very successfully, it's as well to do this *before* bringing it into the house to infest other furniture); and that, after you've spent many hours working on its renovation, it won't look exactly what it is – straight out of a junk shop!

The pictures here show good examples of what can be done. And while it does take a considerable amount of hard work and devotion, the results and the sense of achievement more than make up for it.

Furnishing a living room need not be expensive. Use your imagination to discover the possibilities in old junk-shop finds. The most unprepossessing items can be restored into truly handsome pieces of furniture.

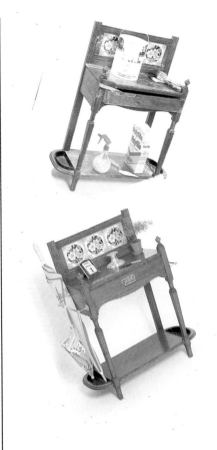

GOOD ASPECTS

Once your decision about furniture is made, you are then in a better position to decide on the overall décor in your living room. You must consider not only the aspect of the room, but at what time of day it is to have most use. If you spend all day away from home and are likely to be out for most of the weekend too, you really want a room for the evening and should decorate and light it accordingly, since the room's aspect is hardly going to matter when you see the room mostly with its curtains drawn.

On the other hand, if it is a daytime room too, you really must take note which way the room faces; a south-facing room will be warm and glowing during the middle of the day and probably gives you more scope in your choice of colours since the effect is going to be light and sunny anyway.

It is a rather different story with a north-facing room. Cool and, maybe, bleak at all times of the day, this room will need visual help to make it warm and cosy. Sunny yellows, perhaps. Cosy red, orange or apricot. All will have a warming affect on a room with a cold aspect. East-facing (early morning sun)

or west-facing (evening sun); you will have to play around with a colour board to mix and match colours and patterns and textures to achieve the effect you most want in the room. And look at the colour board in different light conditions throughout the day so that you will know how the room will vary in appearance at different times.

Designers create their schemes by producing a colour board. A quick sketch of the room, perhaps, or maybe it's easier to stick on a photograph. Collect together colour samples of carpet and fabrics and stick these to the board. See how the patterns mix and match, note the textures, dab on paint colour samples (from those little colour sample pots) – and try out the effects one way and then the next until you have achieved what to you is the most pleasing scheme.

You don't have to follow rigid rules when it comes to colour-scheming. You are trying to find a colour scheme that *you* can live with. So play around with the colours to your heart's content until you've found what pleases you and then go with it with confidence.

GROWING EFFECTS

One of the most effective forms of 'decorating' is with an entirely natural product. It is ever-changing. It needs a little attention at regular intervals. It needs feeding. You must give it a drink on occasions. Best of all you will find it very rewarding. This incredible art form is, of course, the house plant.

It is possible to turn a room into a veritable greenhouse using the variegated leaves for attractive light and shade effects. Look out for large

Many homes lack the luxury of a hall – but still need the services of a hall table. This rehabilitated example makes a virtue of necessity by being attractive as well as practical.

Carefully plan your living-room decor by making up a colour board just as the interior designers do. By assembling samples of fabric, carpet, wallcovering and paint as well as furniture and lighting, you get a good idea of just how well they will all marry up.

floorstanding containers that can be filled with a variety of plants and, if strategically placed near a large picture window, or patio door, will draw the eye to the garden beyond the window. This has the effect of making the room an extension of the garden – or perhaps it's the garden that is the extension of the room.

The concept of extending the garden into the living room is a good one. Visually it creates a feeling of space – important if the room tends to be on the small side anyway. And it prevents the usually hard line between inside and out; a sort of halfway house to the great outdoors. This concept can be furthered by being able to step from your living room into a conservatory with plants and perhaps cane furniture, while the whole garden provides a backdrop.

If you are planning to erect a conservatory, do take care that it is not going to be placed plumb over the only light source in the room. Otherwise your grand idea of having a light, airy extension to your living room could misfire by making the living room itself dark and gloomy. Think this one out carefully before you act.

MOOD CHANGERS

Lights, and the colours and patterns you choose for floors and walls are important elements in changing the mood of the room in a major way. Take lighting first.

There is nothing wrong with a simple pendant light in the centre of the room, but if this is the only light source it will probably have to be very bright to

This amazing living room all but removes the barrier between indoors and out, and makes the most of the splendid garden beyond. The cool ceramic tiles add to the outdoor feel, and the furnishing fabric's pattern is entirely at home with the thoroughly horticultural setting.

If a garden room within the house is not practicable, it may be possible to add on a conservatory to create a similar mood.

Colour with courage: Don't let the long-running vogue for 'background' wall colours such as the off-whites and beiges discourage you from trying schemes as exciting as this sunny yellow – here very much at home with a host of contrasting tones and colours.

In a combined living and dining room, try to position the table close to a suitable serving or storage area. Avoid placing the table in the path of the main traffic route through the room.

provide good lighting in all parts of the room. As a result it may seem harsh and *over*-bright. It is probably better to have several light sources around the room which can be switched on and off individually to give you light exactly where and when you want it.

Attractive effects can be achieved with spots and an uplight. And try to have fitments with heads that swivel up, down and around so that you can turn the light to any direction. Use dimmer switches for low moody lighting; have a pendant light with a down pull sited over a dining table. Place lamps – table or standard – in strategic 'work' areas so that while the rest of the room is moodily lit, you can still read in a pool of good light. Try out coloured bulbs for light with an exciting tint.

While soft lighting effects and attractive furnishing schemes will create a cosy atmosphere, you need warmth, too. You should therefore select your method of heating quite carefully to add to this atmosphere. A room can be adequately warmed by central heating methods, but if you can add to the mood by also having a wood-burning stove or a flame-effect gas fire it will give the room much more style.

If radiators are the only option, look out for the dramatic new hi-tech models that have come such a long way from the original radiator panels. Some have the look of a louvred or venetian blind and come in bright primary colours – very stylish in the right surroundings.

Floors and walls, too, play a large part in the overall mood of the room. A close-carpeted room certainly gives a touch of luxury and has a softening effect. But you don't have to stick to a fitted carpet in one colour. Attractive border effects can be achieved with a contrast pattern, and other types of pattern effects can be created, too. It is not something to launch into with too-cavalier an attitude – you could make some very costly mistakes this way. But with expert design advice you can achieve some stunning and unusual effects.

And that's not the only floor treatment for a living room. Wooden floors in good condition are really beautiful. Treated with stain and

Make every corner of the room count. This corner could have contained just the sofa, but the addition of the table and lamp, along with the picture collection and bell-pulls, turns the area into a special feature of the room.

varnished, with one or two rugs scattered over them, they look as stylish as you can imagine. Painted floors will give a cool, modern appearance. They can also be stencilled with a pretty flower border for an artistic effect. Country farmhouse style comes with quarry tiles and rugs. And for an especially elegant, Italian effect, ceramic tiles can't be bettered.

What about walls? Paint and wallpaper seem to be the first options. Fine. But if they are painted, consider paint effects such as marbling, rag rolling, stippling and so on. And if you are going for a wallcovering, there are a whole host of new vinyl products to consider.

Walls can be covered in fabric (expert advice for their suitability necessary here); while an amazing look can be achieved by surrounding the room with

hanging curtains – almost as if the room's walls were composed of nothing but windows. This treatment is most effective for a night-time room, but just imagine the versatility of a room where you can completely change its appearance by taking down or changing its wall curtains.

Natural colours, a delicate wallpaper frieze, period pieces and flouncy fabrics: vital ingredients for an elegant but comfortable atmosphere for town or country living.

The peachy colour scheme makes this delightful room radiate a sense of warmth and sunshine. The large and exotic yucca plant provides a good contrast for an otherwise cottagey look.

PLANNED LIVING

Since you are very sensibly weighing up the pros and cons of each decision before you go ahead – making a colour board, playing around with lighting effects, seeking expert advice where it's needed – it also makes sense to draw up a proper floor plan of the room. This helps you place, to scale, all your items of furniture in order to save yourself from making mistakes – particularly useful if you are buying new items of furniture since you can check they fit within the room before you buy.

The way to make a floor plan is just as described on page 90 except that in this case your plan is of the living room rather than the kitchen. Working to a similar scale, draw the shape of the room on graph paper, remembering to indicate the windows and doors, and which way they open. Mark in alcoves, the fireplace, radiators and any other immovable items. Note the TV aerial socket, telephone socket and electric points. Try to arrange furniture so such items do not have to be altered.

Still working to scale, make up little cards depicting the exact floor areas of each item of furniture that has to be fitted into the room. Move these around the available floor area until you have a suitable arrangement. Remember that you have to allow for traffic routes so that the family can walk comfortably between key points in the room. You will also need to place seating and tables where there will be an appropriate amount of light – near natural light from the windows, or where there is an electric power point available to plug in light fitments as needed.

Don't forget that just because a room is large enough to take certain pieces of furniture, it is by no means certain that they will go through the doorway, or round the bend in the stairs, so check these dimensions too. You should also check on the most appropriate positions for TV and hi-fi equipment. Before it is set up on a fairly permanent basis, move it around and see what are the most comfortable positions for watching TV to provide both comfort and draught-free warmth. It is also worth installing an extra aerial point so you can move the TV around the room without having cables trailing everywhere. For the hi-fi, you must find the best position for

You don't need an open hearth and grate to create a feature fireplace. This smart wood-burning fire gives a very welcoming look.

Built-in bookshelves can be an exciting feature of any room and can incorporate invaluable storage space in library cupboards beneath.

speakers so that the sound is all you could wish of it.

This is also the moment to make sure you will have adequate storage space in the room. If you are unable to squeeze in enough freestanding storage furniture, look at where you can make extra. A bay window can be converted into a window seat with storage beneath it. Or a short run of seat-high storage boxes can be built along one side of the room which, once covered with comfortable cushions, make good extra seating. Likewise an old pine chest can double up as a coffee table and a storage place for your table linen and place mats, or for old magazines and other bulky treasures.

TALKING POINTS

Every room needs a focal point. In the past, this was often the fireplace because every room had one. Furniture was grouped towards its warmth. But since the widespread installation of central heating in new houses, many builders seemed to dispense with a fireplace entirely, not realising how much their customers really wanted one. So much so, that the York stone people have been doing a thriving trade in stone blocks for homeowners to build their own – even if they were 'dummy' fireplaces complete with log-effect electric fires – in order to have something to sit round!

If you haven't a fireplace as a focal point – and don't want one – create another area in the room as a point of focus. An attractive grouping of furniture, pictures and plants, say. A unit of open display shelving for ornaments, books, TV and other electronic equipment. A stunningly dressed bay window overlooking the garden with window seats and a tumble of cushions.

For other talking points with an individual flavour, create a display from a collection. One of the most striking collections I've ever seen was a wall-mounted display of keys; collected over a number of years, the display spanned keys from all eras ranging in shape and size from huge gaol-like monstrosities to exquisite miniature keys, scrolled and encrusted with semi-precious stones.

Not keys, perhaps? Well, how about commemorative mugs (always plenty of these about from the real old treasures to today's latest offerings). Or toby jugs, or silver salt cellars, or buttons or just about anything. An excellent little book, *A-Z Guide to Small Collectables* by Margaret Edwards, (published by Constable, price £6.95) can guide you in starting up a collection of your own with all sorts of fascinating tips on what to look out for.

ALL-PURPOSE LIVING ROOMS

It is sometimes necessary to make a room serve more than one purpose. Most usually it is when a living room has to perform the service of both sitting and dining rooms. The temptation then is to try and make the room *look* like two

Blue can be the most dramatic of all decorative colours – as this supercool dining room amply demonstrates.

separate rooms – perhaps by using a room divider, or by having a different kind of flooring for each section. Unless the room is L-shaped, thereby providing a natural separation, or has a large alcove off the main area, this approach seldom works.

It is more pleasing to the eye if the room 'flows' easily into each defined area, so avoid 'cutting off' part of a room. This is all-too-easily done if you change, say, from carpet to vinyl tiles or alter the colour and pattern of a wallpaper. This will bring the eye to a too-abrupt halt. Indeed, always remember that this same principle of 'visual jerks' applies to the whole house, so when moving from room to room, allow your flooring or colour themes to lead you naturally from one area to another.

In a small house or flat it is quite common to have a study area included in the living room, though it is better if space can be found in a bedroom where it is easier to work in peace and quiet. When the living room is the only place, try to make the study corner as peaceful and secluded as possible. Install special spot-lighting over a work desk that can double up as a storage cupboard or telephone table, say, when not in use. Soft carpeting will be quieter than other flooring, and all the audio equipment can be fitted with headphones so that it is not disturbing in use – and that means the television, too.

When there are small children about as well, a study in the living room is unlikely to be very peaceful. The answer is to have facilities suitable for children elsewhere in the house. Perhaps a kitchen that is large enough could be arranged to include a play area, or the children's bedroom could become a daytime playroom.

A dining area in an L-shaped living room: pinks and greys help create a clever combination of warmth and spaciousness.

139

A delicately coloured and comfortable scheme for the modestly sized living room in a typical 1930s house. The mouldings, picked out in grey, add an elegant touch to the room.

WELL SEATED

If you are sitting down to read this, spare a momentary thought for the chair in which you are sitting. When it first became a member of your household you may have welcomed it with open arms. It looked really attractive with large comfy cushions and a deep back angle into which you could curl up. But has it really come up to expectations? It is painfully true that very few of us are sitting as comfortably as we should. And this is usually down to the fact that we buy chairs for their attractive contours, fabrics and colours, instead of checking that they will give us the kind of back support that we need.

If a new chair, or chairs, are to be bought for the use of several members of the family, you should all go along to choose. We are all different. A chair that suits a five-footer certainly won't do for someone rising six feet four. And that's not all. Some people get their height from having a long body, others have specially long – or short – arms. All these factors are important when choosing a comfortable chair.

SAFETY WARNING

Some terrifying reports have been seen in the newspapers of people asphyxiated by burning furniture upholstery – and this has happened within a frighteningly short time after the upholstery has first started smouldering. The worst culprits are cigarettes and matches. If yours is a

Chunky oak furniture sits well in this generously proportioned dining room. The paisley furnishing fabric provides an effective unifying theme.

The handsomely formal look of this scheme is helped by the added feeling of height – produced by using a paler shade above the dado rail. The stencilled wall frieze enhances the room's elegance.

'smoking' household, make sure you choose furniture that carries a fire-resistant label. These pieces have passed a fire-resistance test.

All upholstered furniture that has not passed the fire-resistant test must carry a warning label; a red caution triangle. If you buy upholstered furniture with this label, you must take special fire precautions.

FINISHING TOUCHES

It is supremely important to allow your personality to be stamped on the home. Not for you is the carbon-copy tendency of some people to make their homes exactly like the house next door. We have already talked about how changed identical rooms can be by giving them a different design treatment (see chapter

that will theme to your overall decorative scheme. Frames are very often much more expensive than the pictures they surround, so you can either make up your own from the various kits now on sale or make use of old frames from bargain pictures picked up in your local junk shop. If you have a picture of which you are particularly proud, it is worth having a frame made, though; ask the framer to use a moulding and mount that will suit your decor as well as the picture itself.

There are other forms of wall decoration worth considering too. Mirrors, for example, can be found in every shape and form. A very large mirror can be used to good effect to create the illusion of more space in a small room. Remember that you can quite easily buy mirror glass and frame it in any moulding you want, according to your overall décor.

Another idea is the use of wall-hangings. These don't have to be the lavish and costly tapestries that once were so popular in grander houses; ethnic items such as dhurries – now widely available in furnishing shops – can look sensational, bringing a dramatic sense of colour and warmth to the room.

When shopping for accessories, take with you little snippets of fabric, wallpaper and a dab of paint so that you can mix and match there in the shop – and ask the assistants for their advice.

Go for toning shades, or pick out a single shade from a multi-coloured pattern to draw out the accent colour. Remember how colours will look different in changing light, and the lighting you will find in a large department store is hardly representative of the way you will see a fabric once you get it home! So take samples out into the daylight to see it under more regular conditions.

Complement your colour scheme ideas with toning bunches of dried flowers or personal pieces of pottery or bone china – look for ornaments that particularly please you. Don't overdo these touches, or your home will look like the venue for a jumble sale! And collect together only pieces that you like and can bear to have around you. If you've been given an ornament that you absolutely hate you will be aware how difficult it is to buy for someone else.

5), but another way that you can introduce those touches that are peculiarly your own is through your chosen accessories; those almost neglected items like cushions and lampshades that make all the difference.

Prints, photographs and all manner of pictures can be picked up at reasonable prices – and you can expect to find some that have background or accent colours

DECORATIVE FINISHES

A room's overall statement, its individuality, depends to an
almost total degree on its colour and design concepts. The areas
where this is most evident are the walls, windows and floors.
Plan carefully so that when completed, the room 'feels' right

Decorating with fabric: the pretty
effect of frills and flounces is used
here to the full. Treble-layered
café curtains are echoed by the
wall-hanging at the bedhead, in
the same material as the
bedspread.

REMODELLING YOUR HOME

The vast majority of houses in this
country were built before television
dominated our lives, or children had
personal computers, and when kitchens
always had larders and the bath was
always white. So it is not surprising that
certain homes are sometimes in need of a
little adjustment to suit the modern way
of life.

Some rooms are far too large, others
small and pokey; many will need
sub-divisions or enclosures of some sort
constructed. And those rooms which
have party walls with other properties
may well need soundproofing to contain
or exclude a level of noise which no
previous generation has ever been
forced to cope with.

Fortunately, today's technology
allows you to refashion your house in
almost any way you choose. There are a
mass of different plasterboards,
decorative boards, panels, plywoods –
including fire protective and
weatherproof boards – for practically
any application.

Plasterboards are probably the most
widely used form of wallboard in both
new construction and refurbishment
work. While plasterboards come in
many different grades and finishes, the
standard Gyproc wallboard with a

tapered edge is ideal for the domestic situation. It will provide a flat seamless surface, equal to traditional plasterwork after the correct joint treatment has been completed. This eliminates the need for plastering, which is not only a very skilled job, but is also messy and expensive.

For the Halifax house project, British Gypsum demonstrated just how easy it is to construct a 'stud' wall and dry line it with tapered edge plasterboard. From the following instructions you will see that the whole operation is a straightforward DIY job for the competent handyperson, and commonplace for any builder.

Fixing the frame

First, mark out the position of the partition on the floor, including any door openings, making what allowance is necessary for the doorframe. Mark corresponding lines on the ceiling using a plumb line to ensure they are accurate. Then fix a continuous timber sole plate to the floor along the centre line of the partition, with the sole plate secured at 600mm centres. Then you fix a corresponding length of timber to the ceiling.

Vertical timbers – 'studs' as they are known in the trade – should now be fixed at both ends of the partition and in between at 600mm centres for 12.7mm-thick board. Vertical studs should also be fixed either side of any openings. You mark off and cut each stud individually and fix securely by skew-nailing to the timber plates at the base and head. The studs should be braced with horizontal 'noggings' (another trade term) half-way between the floor and ceiling and these are fixed to the studs by skew-nailing. If any further noggings are required to provide support for surface fixtures such as wall cupboards or washbasins, they should be inserted now

Consider the services you may need to incorporate into the new wall. For power points, the electric cable should run within the structure, not on the surface. This will mean drilling holes through the studs. Power sockets should be fixed to the studs; it is simple enough to cut an appropriate opening through the plasterboard to accept the socket box.

Central heating pipes should also be run inside the structure. And if you plan

to fit a basin at the wall, make sure that drilling through the studs to accommodate larger pipes such as the waste will not cause any weakness in the structure.

Fixing the boards

Cut the boards 12mm shorter than the floor-to-ceiling height and press tight against the ceiling with a footlifter. Keeping the board firmly up against the ceiling, fix vertically to the framing, ivory face out, with the paper-bound vertical edges butted together, and centred over the studs.

Nail the board to each support at 150mm centres with suitable Gyproc galvanised nails which should be positioned no closer than 13mm from the edges of the boards. Drive them home straight until the nail head dimples the surface of the board without fracturing the paper liner.

Now board the other side of the wall in the same way.

Joint and angle treatment

Jointing is easier than it seems. As with any other job, care taken will be rewarded by a really good finished appearance.

The materials required are Gyproc joint filler, joint finish and joint tape; the tools you will need are a jointing applicator, a taping knife and a jointing sponge. All of these items are supplied by British Gypsum and can be ordered from the builders' merchant along with the board.

The work is divided into six stages as follows:

Using the applicator, apply a continuous thin band of the joint filler to the taper at the board joints.

Cut the required length of joint tape and press it into the band of filler using the taping knife. Make sure the tape is firmly embedded and free from air bubbles, but with sufficient filler left under it to ensure good adhesion.

Using the applicator again, follow immediately with another coat of joint filler over the tape to fill the taper level with the surface of the boards. Before the filler stiffens, moisten the sponge with clean water and wipe off surplus material from the edges of the joint, taking care not to disturb the main joint filling. Rinse the sponge before reusing.

When the filler has set but not necessarily dried (after about an hour) apply a thin layer of Gyproc joint finish over the joint, using the applicator. Feather out the extreme edges of the finish with the dampened sponge.

When the first coat of joint finish has set and dried, apply another coat in a broad band over the joint.

Feather the edge with the sponge until the surface is smoothed down and then apply a final coat of joint finish.

Exactly the same principle can be used for dry lining a brick or block wall with the battening secured to the wall. On the other hand, if such a wall needs to be further insulated, special plasterboard, with a thermal insulation layer of expanded polystyrene bonded to it, can be applied to the wall with adhesive and then secured in position with nailable plugs.

Sound Insulation

One thing which can be essential, these days, is to make improvements to the sound insulation between party walls. Unwanted sounds can cause a great deal of discomfort and annoyance and the illustration below shows you in what sort of ways all that noise can pass between connecting houses.

THE NOISY NEIGHBOUR

Life today is a jungle of sound: transistors, hi-fi, television, aircraft, traffic and machines. This series of booklets has been written with your comfort and your health in mind. Each day seems noisier than the one before and it is becoming more and more difficult to find that bit of essential peace and quiet. Unwanted sounds cause a great deal of discomfort and annoyance anywhere, but nowhere more so than in the home. In a detached house you may only be troubled by noise from outside, such as traffic or aeroplanes or your own home environment. Where the houses are connected to one's neighbours the situation can be reached where their noise is inflicted on you.

If the brickwork of a party wall has deteriorated and there are any direct air paths through the wall, *however small*, it will allow the passage of sound. The answer is to seal up all direct and indirect air paths and then build a plasterboard wall alongside the existing wall, *but not touching it*, and hang a sound-absorbing glass wool or mineral wool blanket throughout the cavity between the two walls. It is essential the *two* layers of plasterboard are nailed to the timber framing and that the second layer is staggered so that the joints of the two layers do not coincide.

There is no point insulating only one wall – such as in the living room – because for the treatment to be fully effective you must tackle the whole area of the party wall – upstairs as well. Otherwise, vibrations from an untreated wall will transmit sound into the room where the wall has been treated. The whole operation is certainly a major one, but the peace and quiet it will produce should fully justify the effort.

THE TIMBER FRAME & PLASTERBOARD TREATMENT

HANDLING THE PROBLEM

Suggested remedial treatment is:
a. Seal up direct/indirect air paths.
b. Build a plasterboard wall, weighing not less than 3½lb/ft (17 kg/m^2) **alongside** the existing wall but not touching it. Between the walls hang glass wool or mineral wool which are sound absorbing.
c. Remember to do upstairs and downstairs to ensure overall efficiency. Carry out all the measures to guarantee best results.

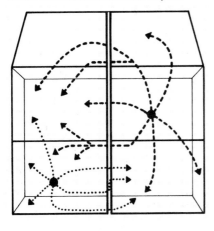

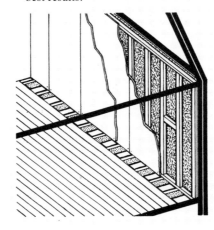

Noggings and fixings

A disadvantage of a stud wall can occur when it comes to fixing things on it. Clearly, anything that is fixed directly to the woodwork is going to be solid, but the plasterboard itself will not withstand more than a modest amount of weight.

It is therefore absolutely essential that if you plan to fix something heavy, like a shelf or a wall-mounted basin, to the wall, you should ensure that there are sufficient noggings built into the framework to give a proper fixing in just the right position.

For lightweight pictures an ordinary steel pin hanger tapped through the plasterboard will normally be quite adequate. However, for heavier mountings on the walls you can choose from a wide variety of fixings which are screwed through the plasterboard and then tightened up against some form of flange at the back of it.

If the plasterboard has been battened to a solid wall you will need a longer fixing device, in order to allow for the gap between the plasterboard and the wall. The Gyproc nailable plug is an excellent means of doing this because it is quicker to install than a screw and stronger than a nail. Consisting of an expandable nylon plug and a bright zinc-plated steel nail, it has an annular ringed shank and flat head which makes it a very neat device for secondary mechanical fixing.

There is much which can be done by using stud partitions to remodel your house and make better, more efficient use of the space available. But you do need to think it all through carefully, first.

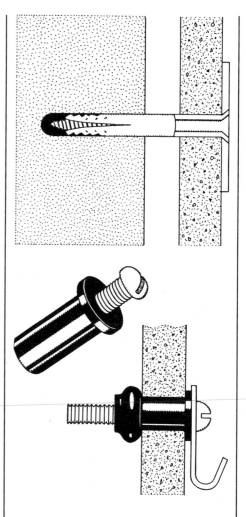

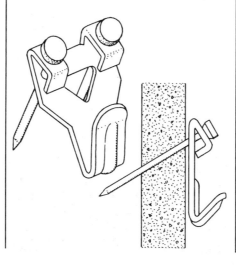

FLOORING

Hard, elegant, soft, cosy, practical and not-so-practical; the choice of flooring comes down to a mixture of what you like, what you can afford, and what is easy to look after. The effects you can create are limitless whatever the choice of material, so it should not be difficult to buy a floorcovering that will suit your lifestyle, and the style of your house. Some people cannot bear to do anything other than whisk a vacuum cleaner over a very large expanse of carpet. Certainly that is a very easy way of dealing with the underfoot part of the domestic chores on a day-to-day, week-by-week basis.

Carpet cleaning is not that difficult as long as it is tackled before it gets too grimy. Shampoo regularly. You can buy or hire a DIY carpet shampooer. Alternatively get in the professionals to do it for you. An sae sent to the Carpet Cleaners' Association, 126 New Walk, Leicester LE1 7JA, will bring you the names of reputable local firms. Some

carpets do have a propensity for showing every mark, and if you have a habit of spilling cups of coffee or walking through with muddy feet, it's best to be expedient and choose a colour and pattern that will not show the marks, or a carpet that has been Scotchgard protected so that most marks are simply shrugged off.

Where to put it

A British Carpets Performance Rating Scheme (BCPRS) has been devised for carpets, and this will help you to choose the right sort for the type of job it is going to have to do for you. Look on the back of the carpet for these categories:

    A.   Extra heavy wear
    B.   Very heavy wear
    C.   Heavy wear
    D.   General wear
    E.   Medium wear
    F.   Light wear

This classification replaces the old numbered system of 1-5.

Wet areas like the kitchen or bathroom must have a carpet that is rubber backed for protection to the floor beneath. Look out for carpets designed specially for these areas.

Quality check

The easiest way for you to check the quality of a carpet yourself is to bend a corner back on itself to see how much of the backing can be seen through the pile. The less backing you see, the better the quality. Alternatively, tug gently at a few of the tufts to see if they are firmly fixed.

Comparing prices from shop to shop can be muddling since there is still a confusing habit of mixing metric and imperial measurements. It's best to get a complete estimate from a couple of shops. Make sure that the price quoted is the *installed* price including underlay, gripper rods and aluminium finishing strips. See whether the store will consider a price reduction if a large

Where fine furniture is a particular feature of a room, it makes sense to add to its emphasis by fitting a neutral-tone carpet. This also helps accentuate the elegance of the scheme.

Some tile manufacturers offer a total, coordinated range with patterned and plans and border tiles – all in matching colour tones. The plain floor tiles opposite could have been substituted by a delicately patterned style such as the floral design on this page.

amount of one type of carpet is ordered.

What type?

Carpets are made in a large variety of man-made fibres and wool or a mixture of both.

Nylon Extremely hardwearing, and it now comes in a huge range of colours. Easily cleaned. When laid, the pile tends to flatten in use. Nylon carpets made with Timbrelle 'S' or Antron 111 are ready-treated with anti-static, which alleviates that old problem of giving mild electric shocks found with untreated nylon carpet.

Wool and nylon The luxury of wool added to nylon gives extra strength and durability to a carpet. The most popular combination is 80 per cent wool to 20 per cent nylon.

Acrylic Wears well. Looks like a wool carpet, but tends to attract dirt. On the other hand, stains are not difficult to remove. Look for an acrylic carpet with high-density pile to alleviate flattening in use.

Polyproplene An extremely hardwearing, easy-clean low-pile type, often used as kitchen carpet.

Polyester Seldom used by itself, this soft fibre is usually used in a blend with other fibres. Attracts dirt, clean before too dirty.

Wool The most luxurious – and costly – material of the lot. It keeps its good looks for many years, doesn't flatten in use and stays clean for longer. Likely to be mothproofed.

The way the pile is cut will affect the overall appearance of the carpet. Cut pile, for example, gives a smooth, dense appearance. A textured look can be given to a carpet with a hard twist pile; that is, yarns that have been given an extra twist before being woven. Loop piles are not cut at all. Although they are hardwearing, the loops can be snagged quite easily and cats' claws can be very damaging to it. If a loop is pulled up, use a crochet hook to try pulling up the flattened one next to it until it's level.

Cutting some of the loops, as in a cut and loop pile carpet, gives extra scope

for an attractive textured pattern. Choose a cord pile in sisal or synthetic fibres for extremely hard wear. It is but another version of a loop pile, except that the loops are very small.

OTHER FLOORCOVERINGS

Ceramic tiles

A smart, long-lasting floor surface that needs little attention. Their fine glaze makes them impervious to water and grease and so they are particularly suitable for kitchen and bathroom. There is a 'but' though. They are cold, noisy and can be tiring to stand on for a long time . . . and if you're a regular butter-fingers, dropped objects may crack or chip the tiles and are unlikely to survive the trip themselves.

Ceramic floor tiles are not that easy to lay properly; a perfectly flat sub-floor is necessary, and if the more unusual-shaped tiles have been plumped for, it could be safer to get the job done professionally. They are quite expensive to buy, but are a dream to keep clean. Just sweep them, and wash occasionally with a mild detergent. Harsh cleansers and brushes can scratch the glaze, so don't use them. and never polish unless you want to end up on skid alley!

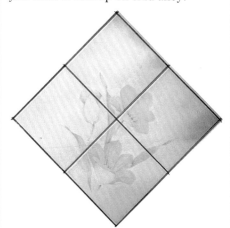

Quarry tiles

With their tough, anti-slip surface, impervious to water and grease, they are suitable for heavy-duty areas like the kitchen, utility room or on a terrace. Their warm farmhouse look is attractive in old houses. Like ceramic tiles, they are noisy, cold, and can be tiring to stand on. The National Master Tile Fixers Association, Fairfax House, Fulwood Place, London WC1V 6DW can recommend professional installers.

The stark, monochromatic effect of this kitchen is artfully softened by the diamond-studded look of the tile-effect vinyl flooring.

Cork

Warm to the touch and soft underfoot. It is also quiet in use. It must be correctly sealed, or stains will penetrate. Not as resilient as ceramic tiles, the edges of cork tiles may chip or crumble and heavy furniture will dent it. It may also fade in sunlight.

Cork tiles sometimes come ready sealed; if yours are not, seal as soon as they've been laid. In a bathroom, seal all over – joins as well – with a coat of varnish to prevent water seeping between each tile. Wash clean, then polish with an emulsion polish. Vinyl-coated tiles are easily cared for with a wipe over.

Linoleum

Once more in vogue, it is a completely natural product made from cork granules and linseed oil and brought to a deep shine with coats of lacquer. Make sure the edges are fixed securely so it doesn't get damaged if it works loose, or allow water to seep underneath causing the lino to rot. Merely wipe clean with a mild detergent.

Rubber

Fire and burn resistant, rubber flooring is available in sheet or tile form, is hardwearing, quiet and waterproof and it is anti-slip as long as it isn't over-polished. It can be difficult to handle if bought in sheet form, so it's as well to call in a professional to lay it for you. Caring for rubber flooring simply calls for a regular sponge-over with warm water.

Vinyl

Over the years, vinyl flooring has been especially popular because of its good-natured temperament. It is resistant to most domestic dangers like water and grease, and if a cushioned vinyl is chosen it is warm and soft underfoot. It doesn't much like heavy objects dragged across its surface and cheap vinyl may begin to wear quite quickly.

A vinyl floor sealer will give a scuff-resistant surface. When this needs replacing (which it will after a while), the original sealer can be removed with wire wool and white spirit before applying a new coat. For day-to-day upkeep of a vinyl floor, wash and rinse well.

Floorboards

If the floorboards are in good condition, there is nothing more attractive than leaving them uncovered in all their glory, though they may be noisy underfoot. You'll first need to sand and seal them.

Wood floors can look magnificent in numerous different guises. Floor paints, varnishes or polishes produce a dramatic range of decorative effects.

Start by scraping off any old lino or vinyl or other substances adhering to the surface. Remove any projecting nails, either by pulling them out with pinchers or by hammering them well under the surface with a punch. If there are any draughts coming up between the floorboards, seal the gaps by preparing a mixture of sawdust and woodglue – or *papier maché* – which you apply as a self-adhesive paste. Very wide gaps should be stopped with thin strips of wood.

Hire a large-belt sanding machine and a small edger. Seal off doors and windows with dust sheets. When the sanding is done, treat the wood with several coats of clear seal to keep its natural colour, or colour it with a wood tone stain or one of the numerous rich colours.

To care for floorboards, sweep, then buff up with a mop and polish.

Woodblock floors

These have a similar warm appearance to floorboards, though they can swell and lift if exposed to extremes of heat or damp. Over the years a woodblock floor will gain a patina that's most attractive. Sweep, mop and emulsion-polish occasionally to keep it looking good.

COLOUR CO-ORDINATION

If there were hard and fast rules in planning a colour scheme, we would presumably all end up having rooms looking exactly like our neighbours. It is somewhat obvious that this is not the case, just as it is evident that some people are much better at working out a colour scheme than others. Some people do seem to have a natural gift of choosing colours and fabrics that tone and blend or contrast, while others, it must be said, appear only to distinguish themselves by the notable disharmony of their schemes.

A whole mystique has been built up around colour scheming and how it can change your life for better or worse, yet it is only necessary to consider a few simple, commonsense points – such as the aspect of the room (namely whether it faces north, south; and whether it is to be used as a living, dining or working room). But in the end, all that really counts is what you like. If the room pleases *you*, that is all that matters.

The somewhat sombre effect of this dark wood panelling is cheerfully contrasted by the fresh cottagey style of the curtains and the cool blue of the paintwork.

KNOW WHAT YOU LIKE

It's no good anyone telling you what colours to use if they are out of tune with your tastes and preferences. You should do your own detective work to determine what moods and textures and colour tones you feel will best suit your home.

Scour through the home interest magazines, visit department stores that display roomsets for you to browse through, look over the manufacturers' brochures for ideas, go to home interest exhibitions . . . and don't be embarrassed to pick up successful decorating ideas when visiting other people's homes – they will be flattered.

You soon know by way of your researches what you find pleasing, and what you would not give house room to. You'll learn, for example whether you prefer sugary 'bright' pastels, or dark 'oppressive' tones. Some colours and patterns may be too dazzling to be restful on the eye.

On the other hand, you may feel most comfortable surrounded by warm sunny yellows, or cool pale blues or restful garden greens. This discipline will help you make a careful choice of scheme, and stop you from making an impetuous decision that you'll regret, perhaps for years to come.

WHAT ASPECT?

The direction a room faces will affect its overall feeling. Does it face the morning sun? If it does, it will cool and dim as the day wears on. A south-facing room will get the best of the day's sunshine while a west-facing room takes on an attractive glow as the late afternoon sunshine shafts through the windows. A north-facing room can be difficult. That's the one that receives no sunlight at any time of the day, and unless you're careful with your colour choice, can seem cold and cheerless. Artificial light will make a marked difference, so a room that will most usually be used at night should be colour-schemed accordingly.

COLOUR AND PATTERN

The clever use of colour and pattern can change the appearance of a room. Visual tricks can be used to great effect to convince the eye of more height, or width or light – or less of these.

IF A ROOM IS CLAUSTROPHOBIC
It would probably benefit from a 'higher' ceiling. Remove any picture rail, paper walls with vertical stripes. Give ceiling a pale, neutral colour.

IF A ROOM IS TOO 'TALL'
Paint ceiling in a deep colour to 'lower' it, taking colour right down to the picture rail. If you have no picture rail, create the same effect with a paper border. Match floorcovering to ceiling. Leave the main part of the walls a much lighter, neutral shade.

IF THE ROOM IS NORTH FACING
What it needs is warmth. Try soft terracotta shades, dusky or salmon pinks, sunny yellows. Natural wood and brick, combined with soft furnishing textures, will also give a warm effect.

IF A ROOM IS SOUTH OR WEST FACING
Cool, spacious minty green, blues and greys will give a light and airy feel to the room. Shafts of summer sunshine will make these colours look stunning.

IF THE ROOM IS TOO LARGE
Break up a large expanse with scattered rugs and pretty screens. Cornices and other decorative moulding help to break up a room, too – especially if contrasted in a different colour tone. A wallpaper border will reduce the ceiling height.

IF THE ROOM IS LIKE A CORRIDOR
Try painting the two long walls in a pale colour, the short end walls dark. This should boost the feeling of width in a long, narrow room.

IF THE ROOM IS VERY SMALL
Go for light colours and maintain the continuity of colour between each area of a room. Don't allow your eye to be drawn to a halt by a sudden stark splash of alien colour.

PAINTING

It is amazing the transformation that can be achieved in a gloomy room by giving it a lick of paint. Relatively speaking, it's

Flouncy festoon blinds relieve the stark lines of a kitchen.

Customised decor: here the stencilled pattern has been picked out from the design on the quilt.

Traditional styling, in soft greens and greys and burnt orange: a formula for a truly restful room.

not over-costly; certainly not compared with re-carpeting, or buying new funiture. And it is easy to do, and quick to complete.

But sloshing paint on to walls and paintwork is by no means the whole story. Effects can be achieved with paint that give the term a whole new meaning. Special techniques with paint are not that difficult to master.

It may take a little courage to roll rags on your newly painted, still wet, surfaces – or to dapple a sponge over it – but once the pretty effects are seen, confidence grows and more daring experiments take place; like paint dragging, or sponging with a contrast colour, or stencilling. Indeed, delicate dado borders can be hand-painted around a room this way to stunning effect.

Floors, too, can undergo an amazing metamorphosis. Wooden floorboards can be painted in startling colours using coloured floor varnishes; bright reds and blues will form the base for a smart new hi-tech room. Stencilled patterns in several colours can be applied to floorboards to dramatic effect. It is possible, of course, to buy ready-made stencils, but perhaps you should take this opportunity to make a stencil to your own design – say a pretty flower border – so that the whole job is truly your own original work.

The same creative work can be applied to walls and ceilings too. Try making a stencil depicting ribbons tied in a bow, then make a dado border round a room by moving the stencil along as you complete each stretch. Make sure that the stencil is free from paint on the backing side, though, or you will transfer paint smudges that look less than artistic. A pattern for a ribbon stencil is given on this page, simply transfer on to graph paper to the size you want.

Don't stop at walls, floors and ceilings. Paint does a wonderful renovation job on furniture, too, where the same paint techniques can be used to good effect.

Plenty of help is on hand in choosing paint colours and matching or toning shades. Most of the paint manufacturers provide colour cards that also indicate 'what goes with what'. They supply free literature containing hints and tips, and booklets offering colour-scheming

ideas. It is, after all, to their advantage to provide all the help they can since satisfied customers are likely to be so pleased with their handiwork that they'll want to buy more paint to try further decorative schemes.

PAINT TECHNIQUES

Sponging
You will need two, or perhaps three, toning emulsion paints in matt or silk vinyl finish, and a natural sponge (bought from a chemist). First paint the wall with its base colour and allow this to dry. Cut the sponge to give it a flat surface, then soak it in water. Squeeze nearly dry. Pour a little emulsion into a dish, then press the flat side of the sponge into it. Don't take up too much paint in the sponge. Gently press the sponge on to the ready-painted wall, lift and repeat. Vary the pattern by slightly changing the way you place the sponge on the wall, and giving it a slight twist as you lift it off again.

another colour can be rolled on, if you wish. When the glaze is completely dry, give it a coat of clear matt varnish.

Marbling

You will need glazing liquid and artist's oil (as for rag-rolling). Choose a base colour and up to three darker toning shades, a 50mm paint brush, a couple of fine artist's brushes and cotton fabric.

For the background, apply a coloured glaze with the rag-rolling technique, then cross brush with a paint brush. Allow to dry. Then using a darker shade and one of the fine brushes, zig-zag lightly across the wall following the rag-rolled pattern, aiming to create irregular-shaped veins. Allow to dry. Then if you like, apply a second and third toning shade to build up the varied tones and patterns found in marble. When finished – and dry – coat with polyurethane varnish to protect it.

Dragging

You will need matt emulsion for the base coat, oil-based glaze, or emulsion thinned with water, a paint brush, a dragging brush (with long bristles). Give the wall a base coat of matt emulsion and paint on the tinted glaze. While still wet, 'drag' the surface lightly from top to bottom allowing it to run into other areas that are still wet, or the effect will be uneven. Vary the pattern by swirling or by dragging horizontally across the wall.

Rag-rolling

You will need plenty of clean cotton fabric, a 10cm brush, rubber gloves and a couple of old pans. Buy glazing liquid (from specialist paint outlets), mineral spirit or paint thinner, artist's oil paint in the appropriate shade. Alternatively, use equal quantities of eggshell paint and white spirit. If using glazing liquid, thin down with the spirit or thinner, then mix in the oil paint until you get the colour you want.

First paint the wall with an oil-based eggshell paint and allow it to dry. Then paint the glazing coat on top in vertical strokes, working a small area at a time. Roll the clean cotton into a loose sausage and, while the glazing coat is still wet, work the cotton sausage up the wall. Repeat, overlapping to avoid obvious 'joins'. As the rag becomes covered with paint, re-roll it so that you are always using a fresh piece of fabric while working. You can experiment with the effects by rolling the rag across the wall in different directions. When dry,

An illusion of greater space is successfully created in this small double bedroom by fitting mirrored doors to the wardrobes.

BRUSH TIPS

1. Buy only good paint brushes. The aggravation caused by a cheap, poorly made brush is not worth the pennies saved on it in terms of the quality of the job (and your temper). Hairs shed themselves into the paint, and if you've ever spent the afternoon digging out hairs from smart new surfaces, and repairing the damage, you'll know how frazzled you feel by the time you get cleaned off for supper!

2. 'Paint in' a brand new brush on primer or undercoats so that it is well run in before being used for a top coat. And check that there are no loose hairs before you start.

3. Look after your brushes. Clean them carefully after use – in white spirit or one of the proprietary products if used with gloss paint; in water when emulsion paint has been used. If the brush is to be used again, the professional trick is to suspend it in a jar and allow the bristles to soak in white spirit. Before re-use, rinse out in white spirit, and dry on a clean rag.

PREPARATION TIPS

1. Starting at the bottom and working upwards, wash down walls and ceilings, then rinse from top downwards, to avoid dirty streaks contaminating the area you've already rinsed off.

2. Strip off flaking paint, smooth edges of firmly adhering paint with sandpaper to avoid a hard line when painting over the top. Treat holes and cracks with filler and sand for a smooth finish.

3. Don't paint over existing wallpaper unless it is one of those embossed lining papers, or anaglypta, that are supposed to be painted.

4. If woodwork is new, sand down till smooth, treat knots with knotting solution. Treat cracks with wood filler. Look out for a fine surface filler – ideal for fine cracks, or an over-open grain. Sand all filled areas to a smooth finish.

5. Remove any rust from metalwork with a wire brush, dust off, clean and dry. Coat with the appropriate metal primer before applying top coats.

6. Smooth over gloss paint with soapy wet-and-dry paper, or a sanding block, to give a good key for the next coat. Rinse and dry the surface thoroughly. Make good all cracks and sand smooth.

7. Use stabilising primer when a painted surface is 'loose' or powdery. A coat of stabiliser will provide a surface good enough to paint over.

A first-home living room created out of strong primary colours and some very basic, low-cost furnishings. The overall effect is eye-catching, and comfortable.

PAINT TIPS

1. Take up an equal amount on your brush each time you dip it into the paint by removing the surplus on the side of the can (or paint kettle).

2. Apply paint in small sections in long, up-and-down strokes. Then 'cross-brush' horizontally over vertical strokes, before returning to long vertical strokes again. This will smooth the paint on to the surface and help to avoid brush marks and paint runs.

3. When you move on to the next section, brush over the edges of the area just painted so that you don't end up with a hard line.

4. Not all paints – gel, for example – need an undercoat. But where one is recommended, don't make do without it. An undercoat helps to fill in small defects and provides a good key for a gloss coat. Overall, you'll get a better finish.

5. Paint a room in the right sequence so that paint splashes are minimised. Start with the ceiling, then the walls, followed by the door. Tackle the windows, door frames and skirting boards last.

QUANTITY

You can calculate the amount of paint to buy by measuring up the square metreage to be covered. Then calculate how many litres you need according to your measurements and the type of paint you are using. The following square areas will be covered by 1 litre of paint:

	Square metres (Rate for one coat on normal surfaces)
Gloss	17
Non-drip gloss	12
Silthane silk	12
Matt vinyl emulsion	12
Silk vinyl emulsion	11
Solid emulsion – matt	12
Solid emulsion – silk	11
Undercoat	15

WALLPAPER

Applying wallpaper makes an instant transformation in any room. With a whole range of qualities and prices available, it need not be expensive to rethink your colour scheme. Manufacturers are constantly bringing out new designs, so with a day or two's work, you can have the very latest styles and textures for your walls.

For some time now, a major trend in wallpapers has been co-ordination. Collections of wallcoverings with matching fabrics can be found in abundance – some manufacturers also including a range of bedlinen in matching colours and patterns.

A host of co-ordinated design packages in florals and pretty rural tones have dominated the 'Country Diary' market. Popular too are stripes and medallion patterns in rich jewel colours which can be found along with the trendy innovation of blown vinyl wallcoverings. This clever technique gives an embossed appearance to

The vinyl papers are the best bet if you are likely to need to scrub the surface clean. Or try the lightly foamed polythene covering known as Novamura. It's easy to hang and just as easy to strip off. Indeed, there is one story (reputedly true) of a customer who liked her Novamura-clad wall so much that she removed the wallcovering strip by strip and rehung it when she moved house!

PREPARATION TIPS

1. Wash down walls thoroughly to remove any remaining scraps of old paper and paste.
2. Fill cracks and rub down. Fine hairline cracks will not show if unfilled so long as a lining paper is used before the wallcovering.
3. Allow newly plastered surfaces to dry out completely before covering with wallpaper.
4. Rub down previously painted surfaces with sandpaper to provide a good key. Make sure that no loose paint remains and that all edges are smoothed over.
5. If covering an oil-painted wall (gloss for example) it is best to hang a lining paper (horizontally, without overlapping the joints) to help the new coverings to adhere properly.
6. All other surfaces whether paint covered or plastered, should be brushed over with a weak solution of wallpaper paste. This is known as sizing.
7. Ask your retailer for help when buying paste – he will know what is most suitable for the type of wallcovering you've chosen. A vinyl covering, for example, needs a paste containing fungicide to protect it from mould growth that sometimes appears when moisture is trapped behind its impervious surface.
8. Use a plumb line to establish a vertical line when hanging wallpapers. This is a length of string with a weight at one end. Simply chalk the string, pin it to the top of the wall (weight end to the floor), hold the line taught and draw it away from the wall. Then 'ping' the string, and it will leave a vertical chalk mark on the wall.
9. Hang ceiling paper first, working away from the window.
10. If your paper is plain, or has a small pattern, start hanging it from the window into the room. Centre the motif of a large patterned paper on a fireplace wall and work outwards from there to draw your eye to the room's focal point.

Coordinated effort: wallcoverings and furnishing fabrics to match are now available in countless styles and patterns. Handled with care, the coordinated look can be very pleasing indeed.

wallcoverings created from expanded vinyl. The surface gives insulation qualities superior to wallpaper. Designs are found in soft pastels, abstracts and geometric patterns as well as the more traditional florals. Popular colour combinations like pink and grey, or turquoise and coral, have ensured their success.

Wallcoverings still abound in their more familiar forms. Traditional papers remain the most common type, and there are washables, embossed papers, woodchips, and flock made either as paper or from vinyl. Vinyl flock, in fact, is the easier to hang and can be washed.

A coordinated theme can be extended by covering doors and drawer fronts of suitable items of furniture.

HOW MUCH TO BUY

WALLS	Measurement round walls, including doors and windows												
Height from skirting													
feet	metres	feet	30	34	38	42	46	50	54	58	62	66	70	74	78
		metres	9.1	10.4	11.6	12.8	14.0	15.2	16.5	17.7	18.9	20.1	21.3	22.6	23.8
7-7½	2.15-2.30		4	5	5	6	6	7	7	8	8	9	9	10	10
7½-8	2.30-2.45		5	5	6	6	7	7	8	8	9	9	10	10	11
8-8½	2.45-2.60		5	5	6	7	7	8	9	9	10	10	11	12	12
8½-9	2.60-2.75		5	5	6	7	7	8	9	9	10	10	11	12	12
9-9½	2.75-2.90		6	6	7	7	8	9	9	10	10	11	12	12	13
9½-10	2.90-3.05		6	6	7	8	8	9	10	10	11	12	12	13	14
10-10½	3.05-3.20		6	7	8	8	9	10	10	11	12	13	13	14	15
CEILINGS			2	2	2	3	3	4	4	4	5	5	6	7	7

HANGING TIPS

1. Ceilings are not the easiest places to reach, so make sure you are standing on a sturdy, secure platform. A plank simply laid between two chairs will not do. A pair of sturdy step ladders is best, with scaffolding boards resting through the rungs. Make sure it is secured before you step on it.

2. To hang ceiling paper, paste a length, then fold it into a concertina. Support the folds over your arm and slide the end in position. Brush over. Then allow the paper to unfold gradually as you work your way across the width of the ceiling.

Hanging ceiling paper is made very much easier if there are two of you. One person positions and brushes the paper on while the other holds up the folds – supported if necessary for height by a broom.

3. For walls, hang your first piece alongside its plumb-lined chalk mark. Brush outwards gently but firmly to remove air bubbles.

4. At ceiling edge and at the skirting board, brush into the angle and draw the back edge of scissors across the paper to mark the cutting line, then, very gently, peel back the unwanted paper and trim off neatly. Clean off any surplus paste.

5. Cut your second, and subsequent, lengths of paper so that the pattern exactly matches the piece already hung even if this means wasting a few inches in order to get the match right. Always butt lengths; if you overlap, the bump will show.

Corners

6. Never try to wallpaper round an internal corner since they are rarely 'plumb'. From the edge of your last-hung piece of paper, measure the distance to the corner at half a dozen places. Add an inch or so to the greatest measurement and cut the next length of paper to this width. Hang this length – it will leave you just enough paper to smooth into the corner.

Use the off-cut to hang on the opposite angle of the corner, allowing it to slightly overlap the first piece. Work on the same principle when papering an external corner.

Light switches

7. Turn off power at the mains. Brush the paper over the light switch and gently crease it round the switchplate. Pierce the paper in the centre of the creased area, making diagonal cuts to each corner. Trim each flap back to about a centimetre and tuck this under the loosened switchplate. Brush down and retighten switchplate.

WINDOWS

Think of a curtainless window – imagine how bleak and bare it looks even if the rest of the room is fully furnished. Curtains or blinds are a major decorative feature of any room, as well as a source of privacy. When drawn, curtains have another important function, too, in helping to keep a room warm, especially if the windows are only single glazed.

Your choice of window dressing will say a lot about your personality. If you are a neat, practical person, you are unlikely to go for the flamboyant frills and swirls. Smart, no-fuss blinds will suit you better, or simple patterns or plains with neat headings.

But within the range of styles, patterns, and your own personal preference, consideration must also be given to the type of house. Is it old or modern? Does it have certain features to play down or dress up? Are the rooms large and spacious, or small and 'boxy'? All these things must affect your choice.

When a room faces into the street, consider doing what many restaurants do: put up café curtains so you can have natural light, and passers-by cannot peer in.

Very modern, geometric patterns will look strange in a really old house that demands a more chintzy, floral appearance. Tiny windows need decorative treatments to make them appear larger. A beautiful bay window can be dressed up into a veritable feature of the room. Choice of pattern, however, must take into account the size of the room because, if very small, a large dominating pattern will absolutely swamp it.

Buying the fabric

Never skimp on the amount of fabric you buy. Curtains that are eked out across the window look, well, eked out. You will never be happy with them. It is better by far to buy lots of inexpensive material than to buy too little of a quality fabric. If, though, you simply must have the fabric you really can't afford, cheat by making up dummy curtains, either artfully draped in the modern swirly fashion or straight, full length dummy curtains that are not designed to be drawn. For night-time, simple, co-ordinating roller blinds can be pulled down over the window for privacy.

To work out your fabric requirements, allow for a fall of curtain to ½in short of the window sill, or ½in short of the floor. Make fabric allowances for hems, headings, and pattern matches.

The chart below guides you to the amount of fabric required for the alternative headings – but these are minimum requirements. If you can run to more, so much the better.

HEADING	MINIMUM FABRIC AMOUNT
Gathered	1½ to 2 times the track length
Pinch pleats	twice the track length
Pencil pleats	twice the track length
Nets	to the main curtain allowance, add 1 track length more. Nets need plenty of fullness.

Extra-long, elaborately draped 'swag and tail' curtains are very popular, but do consider what a lively pup, or a young child could do to them in the winking of an eye. Café curtains are a cosy, practical idea that affords privacy without blocking the light and will also have the effect of 'lowering' a high ceiling. So,

too, will a long valance hung from ceiling height to cover the curtain headings. For a narrow window, extend the pole beyond the window area on both sides, and allow the curtains to hang against the wall, allowing the full width of the window to be uncovered. For a tiny, corner window in a dark room, place a mirror on the opposite angle to the window, thereby reflecting all available light. Hang a curtain on only one side of the window away from the corner so that, when reflected in the mirror, it gives the impression of a total corner window.

Heads you win

Your choice of curtain tape will affect the overall appearance of the curtains:
Standard tape This gives a pretty, evenly gathered look, specially suited to plain fabrics and simple country designs.
Pencil pleat tape When drawn up, the tape coaxes the fabric into neat, tightly tailored, 3in pleats. Suitable for lightweight fabrics.
Pinch pleat tape Draws the fabric into regularly spaced groups of three pleats. This tape does not need to be drawn up too tightly or the fabric's pattern will be lost in the folds. Suitable for heavy curtains.
Smocked heading tape (Spantape), creates an unusual smocked heading effect. Available from distributors of Sunway blinds.
Lining tape For use when detachable linings are required. Sew to the main curtain, and use ordinary gathering tape for the lining itself. Hooks from the lining are inserted into a row of loops on the lining tape, while a second row of loops takes the hooks for the curtain rail.

On tracks

You will find a vast choice of tracks and poles available from which to hang your curtains. The poles – brass or wood – are meant to be seen and stand proud from the wall. The curtains will hang beneath them from large rings and should be very easy to draw.

Curtain track, on the other hand, is usually hidden by the headings, or pelmets and valances. Most tracks available are made from a resilient and rustfree plastic, and you buy by the length, each length coming with the right number of brackets and, usually, hooks. A bay window does not cause a

A window becomes a major decorative feature of the room when given a treatment as exciting as this.

problem, since the track will bend round the bay. Given the measurements, some firms will pre-bend their track for you. It is possible to buy adjustable curtain track that simply slots into a window alcove, dispensing with the need for firm fixings altogether. This can be particularly useful in a fully tiled bathroom.

For some good ideas and sound advice on choosing the right tracks, poles and curtain styles it is worth looking out for the new Curtain Track Advisory Centre symbol in shop windows.

Pelmets

Back in favour, pelmets are now being seen again at the best-dressed windows. Quite rightly, too, for they can provide the total look to the finished window and can play their part in making visual changes to the proportions of a window. Curved, arched pelmets will emphasise the overall height of a window, while frilly, flouncy pelmets will soften the look and exaggerate its width. A smooth, sculptured pelmet provides an elegant, townhouse look compared to the country style effect of a fuller, bouncy frill.

An easy way to create a stiffened pelmet is by making a three-sided plywood box to the appropriate size and shape, hang it above the window, and then staple the fabric on to the plywood. Easy when you want a change of fabric and curtains in a year or so's time. Trim or shape the lower edge. Look out for Pelmform, a stiffened, self-adhesive base for pelmets preprinted with five different pelmet shapings. Select one, cut it out along its outline and stick directly to the back of the fabric. Turn back fabric for a neat edge.

Make gathered pelmets by using curtain tape in the same way as you would for the curtains – after all, they are only very short length curtains themselves. Hang them from a separate track attached to a horizontal pelmet board fixed over the window.

Linings

Lined curtains are better protected from the fading effects of sunlight. They are better at keeping light out of a room and also look much better from the outside of the house than the inside-out appearance evident when curtains are unlined. And lined curtains have good insulation capabilities.

BLINDS

The traditional Venetian blind is still a practical and decorative window treatment, but it has been upstaged lately by the amazingly elaborate festoon blinds which are in effect a vertically drawn curtain.

Like curtains, blinds will dress a window as simply or elaborately as you choose. Simplest of all are the roller blinds; a no-fuss, pull-down blind to do a functional job. Roman blinds, too, tend to be practical rather then decorative, but rather than rolling up or down, they hang in flat panels when closed and pull up into tailored pleats. Roman and roller blind kits for making up at home are widely available.

Venetian blinds can be self-effacing in an all-over neutral colour, or can be produced in several contrasting colours to pick out the key colours in a room. Venetians are used in an atmosphere free from condensation and grease, since clinging grease will make them terribly difficult to clean. Venetian blind cleaning brushes are available to whisk dust from the slats, otherwise a good dunk in warm soapy water will do the trick. Vertical Venetian blinds can give an elegant lengthening effect to a

Colour is the key-note where venetian blinds are concerned. There are now striped slats, slats that have a mirrored or metallic finish and slats that are perforated.

window and are useful for fitting on oddly sloping walls.

Festoon blinds (and the slightly fuller Austrian blinds) are pleated at the top then gathered down the length to give a pretty, scalloped, ruched effect. The frilly flouncing is particularly marked when the blind is raised. DIY kits are available for these, too.

TILING

Ceramic tiles have emerged as a whole new art form. With literally hundreds of different designs available from numerous tile manufacturers, the choice appears limitless. A complete story picture can be built up from half a dozen tiles or so; tiles are colour matched so that you can create your own individual designs with toning tiles. Border tiles offer the facility of creating dado or framed effects as well as borders. And you don't have to keep to a standard square, as rectangular, hexagonal and mosaic tiles are also available.

Soft blinds – which pull up in great scoops – are available in an almost limitless range of fabrics from softest voile to heavy velour.

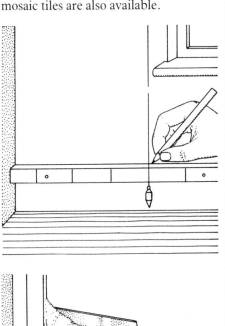

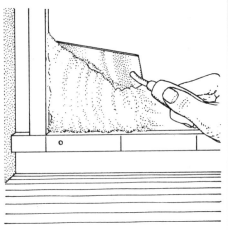

Do-it-yourself tiling is not difficult. But that doesn't mean you can skimp on the preparation work. The surface must be dry, sound, clean and – above all – flat. Obvious? Perhaps, but it's not always easy to detect bumps and dips with the naked eye until you try positioning a tile over it. So use a straight edge to check whether the surface is completely flat.

It is possible to tile over all sorts of surfaces, including::

* existing tiles, provided that they are still firmly fixed
* well-plastered walls
* plasterboard

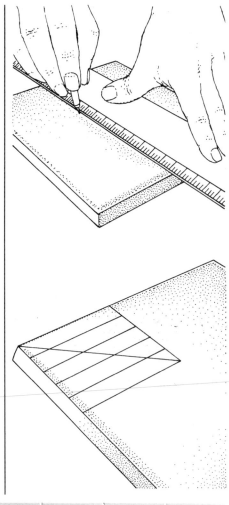

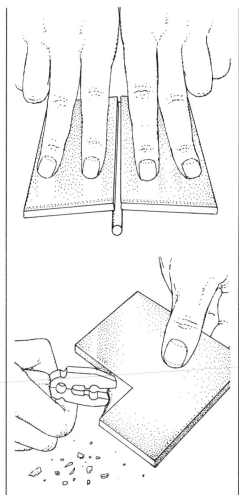

* laminated plastic
* wood, so long as the surface is rigid
* paint, but be extra certain that the surface is well-bonded. Gloss paint should be sanded down.

But, don't tile over wallpaper, even if it does seem to be firmly stuck. Remove this first. If the surface is damaged, repair with filler, dry, then wash the surface down to make sure that it's free of dirt and grease.

Tools and materials

You will need; gauging stick, spirit level, notched spreader, pincers, tile cutter with resharpenable cutting edge, sponge and rubber squeegee. Choose a waterproof adhesive and grout for shower, bath, and sink areas and for window sills. Even better, a fungicidal grout will protect against mould growth. On the other hand, you'll need a heat-resistant adhesive for re-tiling a fireplace. White grout can be coloured with special colourings, if desired.

Plain and simple; elaborately floral; traditional; geometric; tiles that form a complete picture when put together – the decorative effects you can create with today's ceramic ranges are almost limitless in their variety.

OUTSIDE VIEW

Maintaining the exterior of your home makes practical as well
as aesthetic sense – and the same should apply to any alterations
you make to the property's outward appearance

MAINTENANCE

The external appearance and setting of a
house are crucial to its overall worth.
Money spent on keeping the exterior in
trim will make all the difference when it
comes to its 'saleability' in comparison
with other similar-sized properties in the
area. Maintenance is usually regarded as
at best a chore, and something of a drain
on resources; but it is vital if you are to
keep the property in good condition and
protect your investment.

Assuming the house is basically in
good order, the exterior maintenance
will centre on the decorative surfaces
which are constantly under attack by the
elements. While a new or re-tiled roof
should last a lifetime, a flat roof is always
prone to trouble; new or soundly
pointed brickwork will need virtually no
attention, but a painted wall will need to
be redecorated every few years.
Windows, doors and other woodwork
are subject to deterioration too, and it is
just a question of how often you have to
do it.

PAINTING WOODWORK

So far as paint is concerned, the
conventional alkyd gloss system
(primer, undercoat and gloss) used to
protect exterior joinery and cladding is
now being replaced by newer systems.
The need arises from the poorer quality
of wood used in the building industry,
coupled with the generally higher
temperature and humidity levels within
homes (through central heating and
greater insulation) which are causing the
traditional alkyd systems to fail. It is
now generally accepted that any paint
system must maintain at least a 10 per
cent elasticity in order to cope with the
excessive movement that wood
undergoes as its moisture content varies.

The paint industry has, therefore,
taken three different routes as a means of
overcoming these problems. Firstly, the
development of wood stains: you will
find such descriptions as transparent,

opaque, low-build and high-build.
However, it is really only the latter –
often with a high level of pigmentation –
that can protect wood from the effects of
ultra-violet light. Even then, it is
generally accepted that a second
treatment is often necessary within three
or four years. Furthermore, most
woodstains are based on alkyd resins
which soon become brittle and fail
through loss of adhesion in the same way
as alkyd and polyurethane varnishes and
paints fail.

TWO NEW SYSTEMS

ICI, with its brand leader Dulux, have
come up with an oil-based system
which, compared with general purpose
gloss systems, offers at least two years'
added protection. This has been
achieved through a combination of
greater flexibility, the optimum level of
moisture permeability, improved
adhesion and fungal protection.

Fully demonstrated in the *Halifax
House of Home Improvement* video, the
key to the Weathershield Exterior gloss
system is the new preservative primer
which is formulated to penetrate deep
into the bare wood carrying fungicides
to inhibit rot and a binder to stabilise the
wood surface. The exterior undercoat
has a high level of prime pigment for
maximum opacity and the exterior high
gloss is a flexible, oil-based coating
containing a fungicide against
surface-disfiguring moulds.

On the other hand, the makers of
Sandtex decided that the overall
performance characteristics of alkyd
resin (enbrittlement on ageing,
yellowing and chalking) would best be
overcome by producing a water-based
primer/undercoat and a finish coat as a
two-part system, which they have called
Woodshield.

I asked both manufacturers to let me
have their own product ratings in terms
of the application and performance
properties – in comparison with the

Bring all the colour and fragrance
of your garden right into your
home with this tall and airy
conservatory.

By using special preservative tablets (above), wooden windows which have started to rot from lack of maintenance and consequent exposure to the elements can be reinstated. The affected area is first cut out, then treated with a liquid hardener and built up with woodfiller. Holes are drilled to take the presevative tablets prior to redecoration.

conventional alkyd gloss system and low-build woodstain. While only time will tell which of these new generation paints will outperform the other, clearly both have considerable advantages over the traditional method of exterior redecoration.

But what do you do if your windows have started to rot as a result of previous bad maintenance? This is where, on a DIY basis, a wood repair system such as Ronseal's can help restore and strengthen the decayed wood and also prevent further decay. Through the use of a quick-drying liquid hardener, a special resin binds the decayed fibres prior to using a wood filler to build up and repair the wood ready for painting. Ronseal also make preservative tablets which can be placed into pre-drilled holes around areas where moisture is likely to enter the joinery – namely at joints, corners and end grain. This does much to prevent the problem reoccurring.

If DIY is not your strong point, Rentokil provide a specialist service for reinstating rotting windows. The decayed wood is replaced by a special resin filler and the remaining sound timbers are injected with powerful preservatives. The work, carried out by skilled technicians, is guaranteed for 10 years.

Clearly, if your windows are falling apart and the time has come to replace them altogether, this is perhaps the moment to consider the virtues of maintenance-free products finished in plastic. It is for much the same reason that plastic cladding is now replacing wooden cladding, although unless it is used on the most modern of housing it can end up being a maintenance-free eye sore!

Painting walls

So far as masonry paints are concerned, the top two names once again take a divergent view. The Dulux product is based on an all-acrylic resin to give a smooth finish, whereas Sandtex Matt gives a granular textured finish resulting from the mica and fine hard aggregates in a water-borne base. If you want to cover the lines of brick- or blockwork you will find that Sandtex High Build has very good obliteration and is a tough and durable product. It is designed to give a protective coating for a period in excess of 15 years.

While there are many books devoted to interior decoration, the only one which caters wholly for exterior decoration – and should be required reading for anyone contemplating changing the face of their house – seems to be *Your House – The Outside View*. Written by architect John Prizeman, the book was commissioned and sponsored by the Blue Circle Group and aims to help people to understand why houses look the way they do and how we may care for them. It has been meticulously researched and contains many useful photographs and drawings.

Keeping up the roof

A flat roof that is leaking can be a nightmare. It may be obvious where the water is coming into the room, but it is often very difficult to see exactly where the leak is above. Until recently most waterproofing compounds were bitumen based and, therefore, degraded with the ultra-violet in sunlight, so that even if you managed to 'patch' your way out of the problem it would certainly not last for a very long time. However, a recent product on the market appears to have supplied a solution. Called Isoflex, it is a high-performance urethane elastomer that is permanently flexible and when applied to almost any roof surface will cure to a tough, highly adhesive waterproof membrane. It is used with a special primer, as well as a special clean-up fluid to wipe away drips and splashes as well as cleaning your brushes.

Other common maintenance jobs include working on wooden fences, potting sheds and garden furniture, together with the many metallic items such as ornamental gates, railings, latches, hinges, lamp brackets and a mass of other things that rust and corrode so enthusiastically in our climate. Once again, there are some very good products on the market for dealing with all these and many of the other nagging chores that come with home ownership.

For years, there was no better answer than creosote – and it still does a very good job. But it is not pleasant to use and has the sort of smell that really does get up your nose! It was therefore only a matter of time before an alternative product appeared. This is a water based product called Fencelife, which is harmless to both plant life and animals and it doesn't smell.

Another useful product is Hammerite, a metallic paint which can go straight onto rusty metal without the need for a primer or an undercoat. Three years ago I painted our rusty old weather vane with Hammerite and – while I'm not climbing up there again for a close inspection – from the ground there doesn't appear to be a rust spot on it.

When you shop around for these longer-lasting types of maintenance products you will find they are more expensive than their traditional counterparts. But even if you double the price of a can of this or a can of that, if it really does mean not having to redo the job for a couple of years or so longer than before, it must be very worthwhile. If nothing else it leaves a lot more time for the more pleasurable pursuits – and for many of us, that means more time to conjure up ideas for further improvements and minor developments to the property.

An all-glazed bay provides a fine outlook on to a glorious garden – and also brings welcome natural light into the room inside.

ADDITIONAL AMENITIES

Most people who buy an older property do so because of its maturity; they are drawn by its features and setting. Very often it is the older property which has the greater potential for further development – both inside and out. Naturally, the amount of land surrounding the house and particularly the access to it, determines just how much can be done. Often however it is just a question of scale.

A small terraced house in town, with only a few feet of garden at the front and a small rectangle to the rear, will naturally have particular restrictions that a semi in the suburbs with more leafy surroundings will not have. Both, for example, might want a conservatory, but one of necessity may have to be somewhat smaller. What may be a wholly paved front area for one may be but a patio as part of a large back garden. A tiny ornamental pond in town or a rather more elaborate affair in the country: both have to be designed and

built with equal respect for their setting.

In some ways, developing the outside of a property can be much more difficult than improving the inside. While everyone likes to have their own individual points about a kitchen, there is a certain logic which is accepted by most; bathrooms may be appointed in all manner of different ways, but they do all have to have certain sanitaryware to

A well-sited conservatory makes enjoyment of the great outdoors a year-round pleasure.

At the front of the house, particularly where cars will stand, block paving makes a long-lasting and attractive surface.

A sunroom in the grand manner: the current vogue for conservatories means that the range of designs on the market has become wide enough to suit just about every size and style of home.

function at all. But a garden – so called – can actually mean anything to anybody!

Recently, I visited a friend in London who had just moved into a Victorian terraced house in some unheard of postal district that was now the fashionable place to live. I suppose the house cost £200 to build and now cost three more noughts to buy. The front door was six strides from the pavement and the back garden something less than double that in length – but with the neatest, greenest grass I've ever seen. 'I'm building a conservatory right across the back,' I was told 'and paving the rest.' Knowing the person concerned very well, I know it will all be tremendous when it's finished – and there will be more green in the conservatory than there was grass on the lawn!

DRIVE-IN MERITS

Given the space and the access, a garage must be high among most people's priorities these days. To build what was first called a 'Motor Car House' would be a considerable investment, but there is no doubt that the modern prefabricated structures with pitched or tiled roofs are very acceptable alternatives. However, remember it is well worth the marginal cost of ordering a larger garage than you might need, strictly speaking, for the size of car you are going to keep in it. The additional space for garden equipment, workbench, freezer, bicycles, and so on is invaluable. And if it can be sited at least five metres from the house, its erection will not count as part of your 'permitted development' allowance.

As described in Chapter 2, you can cover half the area of your garden with small structures so that you have a mass of different options for putting up sheds, greenhouses, summerhouses or even a sauna cabin. The latter is particularly desirable if you are considering putting in an open-air swimming pool.

SWIMMING POOLS

When my wife and I bought our near-derelict, isolated, Victorian gamekeeper's cottage we found to our amazement that a small outbuilding had a complete Finnish sauna installed. Bearing in mind that at the time there

was neither water nor electricity laid onto the property, it did seem an unusual refinement. Having installed the necessary services, we did decide to put in a small swimming pool – partly as a certain means of having a reservoir of 14,000 gallons of water in case of fire. Subsequently, we find that the swimming pool is only pleasurable – with the sort of weather we get in this country – because of the warmth of the sauna as a means of revival.

While an open air swimming pool in the right size of garden can create a marvellous setting, it is a relatively expensive hobby for the few days a year that a typical British summer will allow you to enjoy it. A covered pool may extend the swimming season, but the heating costs are a significant factor to be taken into account. So is maintenance, for even in the depths of winter the pool needs attention.

EXTENSIVE INTERESTS

Conservatories, greenhouses and porches are all very popular additions to a property. While all three have been made exempt under the new Building Regulations for building control

A swimming pool looks best if it appears to be a natural part of its garden setting. But don't expect a pool to be anything other than very expensive to install and maintain.

purposes, you will find that the planning situation is different for each one.

While a conservatory which is attached to your house and approached from it is clearly an extension of the building, and a greenhouse at the bottom of your garden is equally clearly a separate structure, what is the position over a lean-to glazed structure against a wall of the house but which can only be approached from the outside? Is it a greenhouse and therefore part of your allowance for covering 'up to 50 per cent of your garden area with small structures' or is it likely to be classed as an extension to the main building and therefore part of the 'permitted development allowance' for enlarging the property?

This is where, unfortunately, you may find that one local authority's interpretation may be completely different to that of another's, but usually such anomalies are finally determined by the Department of the Environment. Naturally, if you have used up whichever section of your development rights is deemed to apply, you would have to submit a planning application in any case.

So far as a porch is concerned, once again, within the limitations described in Chapter 2, you have a right to build one at any external door – over and above your other permitted development allowances.

There are a considerable number of manufacturers producing a whole variety of different prefabricated designs for all three types of glass structure. Some have wall panels and fascias which make them appear to be much more of a home extension – but as long as the structure has a translucent roof it can be classified as a conservatory and so be exempt for building control purposes. Virtually all manufacturers of these prefabricated structures emphasise the fact that the doors and at least the lower glazed panels will be of safety glass and most recommend the virtues of double glazing.

OUT ON THE PATIO

The adding of a conservatory opening out from a living room or dining room to the rear of the house usually heralds a patio of some sort. While plain solid concrete – as an extension of the slab on

The conservatory-patio combination has many shapes and forms, but all achieve that marvellous magic of bringing house and garden together as one.

A stonework terrace provides a natural junction between house and garden.

Decorative brickwork can give an exciting extra dimension particularly to a garden that is all on one level.

which the conservatory is erected – is an economic way of producing a patio, a much more interesting and attractive approach is to use reconstituted stone paving which is now available from builders' merchants and garden centres in a wide range of sizes, finishes and colours.

Compared with the slabs you find on pavements, they are light and easy to lay and the major manufacturers produce walling blocks and screen walling to coordinate.

Whether you have a large or small garden, you will find that it is the architectural features which help to make it individual – and there is no doubt that stone is the perfect complement for nature's greenery. In fact, once you get going with paving in your garden you will find that project will follow project, because the possibilities and permutations are almost endless. And the beautiful thing about stone is that almost whatever you do, the end result is not only very pleasing to the eye, but is also virtually maintenance-free.

PAVING – THE WAY

Any paving which is to be immediately adjacent to the house should be laid below the level of the damp proof course. It should slope very slightly away from the house to ensure that the rainwater runs away from it. The fall should not be less than 1in in 5ft and you should make sure that the edge of the paving where it meets the lawn should be at a slightly lower level than the grass to make it easy when doing the mowing.

Having marked out the site with pegs and string lines, adjust the top of the pegs to establish the finished level of the paving. Then excavate this area and refill with 3in of hardcore. Thoroughly ram down and finish with a 2in layer of sharp sand. Working with a mix of semi-dry sand-cement mix using 1 part cement to 4½ parts concreting sand, start in a corner by placing a good-sized dab of mortar at each corner of a slab and one for the centre. Then, position the paving and tap it down with the wooden handle of a hammer and check for accuracy with a spirit level.

Using small pieces of wood as spacers, maintain the gap for the joints between each slab and work diagonally across your site. Every so often check the fall away from the house with a length of straight-edge and a spirit level.

There are two ways in which you can finish the joints. One is to point with a stiff, wet mortar and, using a wooden jig (*overleaf 2*) to protect the surface from staining, press into place with a pointing trowel. Alternatively, make a dry mix of 1 part cement to 4½ parts concreting sand and brush all over the paving to fill all the joints. Then, with a watering can

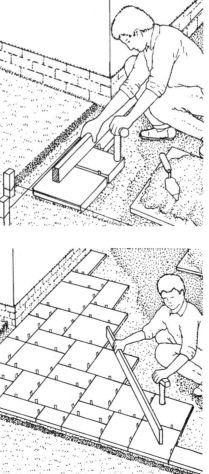

Paving makes all the difference to a garden, and laying stones is a simple and pleasurable do-it-yourself project.

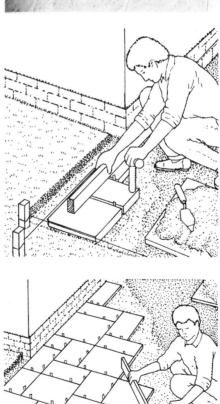

It is vital that paving should fall slightly away from the house to ensure rainwater runs off. When laying paving, check for an even fall using a block set under your straight edge and spirit level.

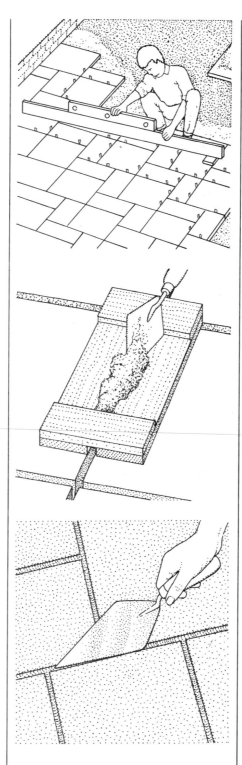

To point slabs with wet mortar, make a simple jig with wood offcuts and with a gap the width of the joins. Compact the mortar into the joins with the edge of the trowel. Remove the jig, then rake the joins with a pointing trowel before the mortar sets.

fitted with a fine rose go over the whole surface. A certain amount of settling will occur, so that the process will usually have to be repeated – but it saves a lot of backache!

Where you want to lay paving which is likely to be subject to heavy traffic, such as at the front of the house for a driveway, it is best to use the more substantial block paving. In the *Halifax House of Home Improvement* video Countryside Masonry were asked to demonstrate the way this is done using their very durable Europa rectangular block paving. While the blocks can certainly be bedded in by hand, you will get a very much better result by hiring a mechanical plate vibrator (and at the same time hiring a mechanical block splitter).

The foundations must be firm and a hardcore base of at least 4in thick is recommended. On top of this is laid a 2in layer (after compaction) of sharp sand and a further 2in must be allowed for the blocks, which of course will be bedded by compaction into the sand. A herringbone pattern will give added strength and interlock more easily when laying.

During the laying it is important to lay planks across the work to carry barrows and avoid the shifting or tilting of the blocks which have been laid, but not embedded. The vibrator is passed two or three times over each complete section, but make sure that it stays at least a metre away from the laying face. Finally, a thin layer of fine dry sand should be spread over the blocks and, using the vibrator again, a second person keeps brushing the sand under the leading edge.

Countryside Masonry have produced a helpful 48-page *Book of Garden Ideas* with concise instructions on how to do everything. The booklet is well illustrated, and shows you exactly what tools and materials you will need as well as how to prepare foundations, levels and falls, build walls, steps, raised flowerbeds and a mass of other features.

Another manufacturer, Bradstone, has brought out an interesting block design whereby you can in effect lay four conventional-sized blocks in one go. Called Aztec, each block appears to have four separate bricks or stones built together in the usual half-bond joint. It would certainly help a novice to build a wall more quickly and easily and there is also a similar brick-on-edge coping, for completion.

IN THE WET

A pond is a marvellous feature to have in a garden and you can derive a lot of personal satisfaction from designing and producing your own. Furthermore, it is the sort of project which can be embellished with time and as your funds permit rather than having to be carried out all in one go. The important thing is to take your time at the planning stage and make sure that you get the basic structure right because, whereas other parts of the garden can be changed fairly easily, once you have installed your pool you are somewhat committed!

There are of course quite a number of things to consider before you start. Do you want a formal, ornamental pond or a rather wild irregular shaped pool? Should it be raised or just sunk in the ground? Do you want lots of plants or not? What about fish? Are you thinking about putting in a fountain or a waterfall? Your answers will have a decided bearing on the shape, size, depth and location, as well as on the materials and equipment required.

A raised pond is generally a more formal structure and it does have the advantage of requiring a great deal less excavation work – plus the problem of disposing of the soil. A raised pond will also provide a seating area along its border and is less of a hazard for the young or the infirm. In fact, with a very young family it can start its life as a sand pit (*containing* the sand rather than letting it spread all over the place, as with a sunken pit) and then be turned into a pool later. If you are not an over-keen gardener, a raised or more formal pond can be incorporated with much more paving around it rather than flowers and shrubs which will inevitably need attention.

A more informal pool is probably best sunk in the ground and, to save a lot of cartage, the earth you dig out can be banked behind it to create a rockery or perhaps incorporate a waterfall. You will also find much more latitude for curvaceous design and it is a great deal easier to produce the overall shape that you want. It is best to begin by laying a rope or hose in the shape you want on the ground and excavate from the inside,

Water adds a very special extra element to a garden. Simple ponds can very often be constructed on a do-it-yourself basis.

Build-your-own pond:

1 Lay a rope or hose to the required shape. Cut inside the outline to allow for final trimming round the perimeter.

2 The excavating is started, leaving marginal shelves where required 9 in wide and 9 in below water level.

3 Check levels by tapping in short pegs right around the pool and levelling their tops with a spirit level.

4 Drape the pool liner in the excavation leaving an even overlap all round. Weight down the overlap before filling.

5 The pool can be edged with broken slabs of paving laid on a bed of mortar, one part cement to three of sand.

Add lilies and other pond plants not just for appearances, but to attract wild life and keep the water from stagnating.

to allow for final trimming, and leave marginal shelves where required about 9in wide and 9in below water level.

Insert wooden pegs 3ft to 4ft apart around the pool. Establish the level with a spirit level because water will find any faults. Finish with a cushion of sand and then drape the liner loosely into the excavation held in place by bricks and start filling with water. As the pool fills stretch the liner to remove creases and gradually ease the bricks off. Trim the liner to leave a 4in to 5in flap securing this by driving 4in nails through the lining to ensure it does not slip.

The pool can then be finished around the edge with paving stones bedded on a 3 parts sand to 1 part cement mix of mortar. Then empty the pool and clean out – making sure that any mortar dropped into it is totally removed. Refill and stock with plants and fish.

The alternative to using a sheet liner made out of polythene, PVC or butyl – the latter being far the best – is a preformed reinforced-glass fibre or plastic semi-ridged moulded liner. They obviously come in many different shapes and sizes, but are often difficult to transport and you will need sand for back-filling after doing your excavation to ensure that it is well supported.

With a submersible pump, you can easily install a fountain and perhaps go on to create a waterfall – or a whole series of them. For some exciting ideas on creating a pond it is well worth studying *The Stapeley Book of Water Gardens*. If

you have the opportunity, visit Stapeley Water Gardens near Nantwich in Cheshire where Ray and Nigel Davies boast the largest range of water garden equipment in the world.

LIGHT SHOW

Gardens – one is tempted to say particularly those with water – can look simply marvellous at night with a few well-placed lights. All the shapes and silhouettes look totally different at night and you get a perspective which cannot be seen by day. On a balmy summer's evening an *al fresco* meal or party outside can be a most enjoyable form of entertaining friends and family. But good outside lighting can do more than that for you; it can help to secure your home.

While stylish coach lamps at the front porch make for a warm and welcoming feeling for your friends and guests, they will also deter an intruder from approaching the house. If you have a passageway down the side of the house, it is also sensible to have lighting there, as well as at the back door. For obvious reasons burglars do not like bright lights and while there is no substitute for proper physical security with your windows, doors and other openings, lighting will help to protect your perimeter.

It is important that the lights you use outside are designed for the job. It is safer and better to have a separate circuit installed which should be isolated and used with waterproof socket outlets. Lights out of doors will seem to be much brighter and should be hidden by a baffle and diffused so you are not dazzled by them.

If you are trying to light up trees and shrubs try a linear tungsten halogen light and, if you can, back light them so that you get a much more interesting effect from the front. You can also light a pond by using low-voltage fittings with coloured lenses. These can either be floated on the surface or submerged. A waterfall can be lit in the same way, using similar fittings.

Using lighting to create the mood and atmosphere you want can be a lot of fun, but it can be difficult to find exactly the light fittings you want. So do spend some time in a major lighting stockist such as British Home Stores to find out just what is available. You should find it an illuminating exercise.

Good lighting makes a garden come alive at night, allowing you to enjoy the pleasures of the outdoors whenever you choose.

185

APPLICATION PROPERTIES

PROPERTY	CONVENTIONAL ALKYD GLOSS	LOW BUILD WOOD STAIN	SANDTEX WOODSHIELD	WEATHERSHIELD EXTERIOR GLOSS SYSTEM
DRYING TIME PER COAT	6-12 hours	1-24 hours (depending on thickness)	$\frac{1}{2}$-1 hour	6-12 hours
RECOATING TIME	12-24 hours	12-24 hours	2 hours for primer undercoat 6 hours for finish	12-24
CAPACITY/COVERAGE	10-15m²/litre	5-20m²/litre	10-15mm²/litre	15m²/litre
EASE OF BRUSHING	Some drag	Easy	Easy	Some drag
EQUIPMENT CLEANING	Needs white spirit	Needs white spirit	Uses water	Needs white spirit
ENVIRONMENTAL POLLUTION	Flammable Solvent oxidation odours Can contain lead dryers		Non-flammable No unpleasant odours No added lead	No lead driers

PERFORMANCE PROPERTIES

PROPERTY	CONVENTIONAL ALKYD GLOSS SYSTEM	LOW BUILD WOOD STAIN	SANDTEX WOODSHIELD	WEATHERSHIELD EXTERIOR GLOSS SYSTEM
ADHESION	Good over most surfaces, poor on damp surfaces	Poor over damp surfaces	Good, not affected by damp surfaces	Good over most surfaces, poor on damp surfaces
FLEXIBILITY	Initially good but rapidly	Initially good but reduces rapidly	Excellent throughout	Maintain at higher level than conventional
GLOSS	Mirror-like finish, reduces on ageing	Normally low	Soft gloss maintained on ageing	Mirror-like finish, reduces on ageing
COLOUR	White tends to yellow	Natural shades only darkness or u/v – maintains whiteness	White not affected by heat,	White tends to yellow
LIQUID WATER PERMEABILITY	Low	High	Low	Low
WATER VAPOUR PERMEABILITY	Low	High	Medium	Medium
TIME TO REDECORATION	3-5 years	Approx 2 years	5-10 years	5-7 years
REDECORATION PROCEDURE	Need to strip off failing areas (failure is by cracking and flaking off)	Need to clean	Need to clean only (failure is by gradual erosion)	Less frequent need to strip off failing areas (failure is by cracking and flaking off)

USEFUL ADDRESSES

ASSOCIATION OF BRITISH
INSURERS
Aldermary House, 10-15 Queen St,
London EC4N 1TT. 01 248 4477.

ASSOCIATION OF BUILDING
CENTRES
26 Store St, London WC1 7BT.
01 637 1022

BRITISH BLIND AND SHUTTER
ASSOCIATION
5 Greenfield Crescent, Edgbaston,
Birmingham B15 3BE. 021 454 2177.

BRITISH CHEMICAL
DAMPCOURSE ASSOCIATION
16A Whitchurch Road, Pangbourne,
Reading, Berks RG8 7BP.
07357 3799.

BRITISH DECORATORS
ASSOCIATION
6 Haywra St, Harrogate, North Yorks
HG1 5BL. 0423 67292/3.

BRITISH FLOORCOVERING
MANUFACTURERS ASSOCIATION
125 Queens Road, Brighton, East Sussex
BN1 3YW. 0273 29271.

BRITISH GAS CORPORATION
326 High Holborn, London WC1V 7PT.
01 242 0789.

BRITISH HARDWARE
FEDERATION
20 Harborne Rd, Edgbaston,
Birmingham B15 3AB. 021 454 4385.

BRITISH INSTITUTE OF
ARCHITECTURAL TECHNICIANS
397 City Rd, London EC1V 1NE.
01 278 2206.

BRITISH STANDARDS
INSTITUTION
2 Park St, London W1A 2BS.
01 629 9000.

BRITISH WOOD PRESERVING
ASSOCIATION
Premier House, 150 Southampton Row,
London WC1B 5AL. 01 837 8217.

BUILDERS' MERCHANTS'
FEDERATION
15 Soho Square, London W1V 5FB.
01 439 1753.

BUILDING CENTRE
26 Store St, London WC1E 7BT.
01 637 1022.

BUILDING EMPLOYERS
CONFEDERATION
82 New Cavendish St, London
W1M 8AD. 01 580 5588.

BUILDING RESEARCH
ESTABLISHMENT
Bucknalls Lane, Garston, Watford
WD2 7JR. 0923 674040.

THE CAVITY FOAM BUREAU
PO Box 79, Oldbury, Warley, West
Midlands B69 4PW. 021 544 4949.

CEMENT & CONCRETE
ASSOCIATION
Framewood Road, Wexham Springs,
Slough, Berks. SL3 6PL. 02816 2727.

CONFEDERATION FOR THE
REGISTRATION OF GAS
INSTALLERS
St Martin's House, 140 Tottenham Court
Rd, London W1P 9LN. 01 387 9185.

CONSUMERS ASSOCIATION
14 Buckingham St, London WC2N 6DN.
01 839 1222.

COUNCIL OF BRITISH CERAMIC
SANITARYWARE
MANUFACTURERS
Federation House, Stoke-on-Trent
ST4 2RT. 0782 48675.

DEPARTMENT OF THE
ENVIRONMENT
2 Marsham St, London SW1P 3EB.
01 212 3434.

DESIGN COUNCIL
Design Centre, 28 Haymarket, London
SW1Y 4SU. 01 839 8000.

DOMESTIC SOLID FUEL
APPLIANCES APPROVAL SCHEME
Hobart House, 40 Grosvenor Place,
London SW1X 7AE. 01 235 2020.

DRAUGHTPROOFING ADVISORY
ASSOCIATION
PO Box 12, Haslemere, Surrey
GU27 3AN. 0428 540111.

ELECTRICAL ASSOCIATION FOR
WOMEN
25 Foubert's Place, London W1V 2AL.
01 437 5212.

ELECTRICAL CONTRACTORS'
ASSOCIATION
34 Palace Court, London W2 4HY.
01 229 1266.

ELECTRICAL INSTALLATION
EQUIPMENT MANUFACTURERS
ASSOCIATION
Leicester House, 8 Leicester St, London
WC2H 7BN. 01 437 0678.

ELECTRICITY COUNCIL
30 Millbank, London SW1P 4RD.
01 834 2333.

ENERGY EFFICIENCY OFFICE
Thames House South, Millbank, London
SW1P 4QJ. 01 211 6811.

FEDERATION OF MASTER
BUILDERS
Gordon Fisher House, 33 John St,
London WC1N 2BB. 01 242 7583.

FIBRE BUILDING BOARD
ORGANISATION
1 Hanworth Rd, Feltham, Middlesex
TW13 5AF. 01 751 6107.

GLAZING & GLASS FEDERATION
44-48 Borough High St, London SE1
1XP. 01 403 7177.

THE GUILD OF MASTER
CRAFTSMEN
170 High St, Lewes, East Sussex
BN7 1YE. 0273 477009.

HEATING PUMP & AIR
CONDITIONING BUREAU
30 Millbank, London SW1 3RD.
01 834 8827. Ansaphone

HEATING & VENTILATING
CONTRACTORS ASSOCIATION
Esca House, 34 Palace Court, Bayswater,
London W2. 01 229 2488.

INCORPORATED SOCIETY OF
VALUERS & AUCTIONEERS
3 Cadogan Gate, London SW1X 0AS.
01 235 2282.

INSTITUTE OF PLUMBING
64 Station Lane, Hornchurch, Essex
RM12 6NB. 040 24 72791.

KITCHEN SPECIALISTS
ASSOCIATION
31 Bois Lane, Chesham Bois, Amersham,
Bucks HP6 6BM. 02403 22287.

THE LAW SOCIETY
The Law Society's Hall, 113 Chancery
Lane, London WC2A 1PL. 01 242 1222.

NATIONAL ASSOCIATION OF
ESTATE AGENTS
Arbon House, 21 Jury St, Warwick
CV34 4EH. 0926 496800.

NATIONAL ASSOCIATION OF
PLUMBING, HEATING &
MECHANICAL SERVICES
CONTRACTORS
6 Gate St, London WC2A 3HX.
01 405 2678.

NATIONAL CAVITY INSULATION
ASSOCIATION LTD
PO Box 12, Haslemere, Surrey
GU27 3AN. 0428 54011.

NATIONAL FIREPLACE COUNCIL
PO Box 35 (Stoke), Stoke-on-Trent,
ST4 7NU. 0782 44311.

NATIONAL FEDERATION OF
ROOFING CONTRACTORS
15 Soho Square, London W1V 5FB.
01 734 9164.

NATIONAL HOME IMPROVEMENT
COUNCIL
26 Store St, London WC1E 7BT.
01 636 2562.

NATIONAL HOUSE-BUILDING
COUNCIL
Chiltern Avenue, Amersham, Bucks
HP6 5AP. 02403 4477.

NATIONAL INSPECTION COUNCIL
FOR ELECTRICAL INSTALLATION
CONTRACTING
Vintage House, 36-37 Albert
Embankment, London SE1 7UJ.
01 582 7746.

OFFICE OF FAIR TRADING
Field House, 15-25 Breams Building,
London EC4A 1PR. 01 242 2858.

ROYAL INSTITUTE OF BRITISH
ARCHITECTS
66 Portland Place, London W1N 4AD.
01 580 5533.

ROYAL INSTITUTION OF
CHARTERED SURVEYORS
12 Great George St, Parliament Square,
Westminster, London SW1P 3AD.
01 222 7000.

ROYAL SOCIETY FOR THE
PREVENTION OF ACCIDENTS
Cannon House, The Priory, Queensway,
Birmingham B4 6BS. 021 233 2461.

SOLID FUEL ADVISORY COUNCIL
Hobart House, Grosvenor Place, London
SW1X 7AE. 01 235 2020.

THE SWIMMING POOL & ALLIED
TRADES ASSOCIATION
Spata House, 1A Junction Road,
Andover, Hants SP10 3QT. Ansaphone.
Consumer enquiries 01 291 3455.

TIMBER RESEARCH &
DEVELOPMENT ASSOCIATION
Chiltern Hse, Stocking Lane, Hughenden
Valley, High Wycombe, Bucks HP14
4ND. 024024 3091.

ACKNOWLEDGEMENTS

The publishers would like to thank the many organisations and people who gave valuable advice and assistance in the production of this book, with special thanks to Ken and Pauline Finn.
Editor Ned Halley
Art Direction/Editing Ivor Claydon
Jacket Design Sunset Design
Typesetting Prestige Press (UK) Ltd
Production Consultant Nicholas Russell
Special Assistance Anne Scutcher

Photographs

A
Abbot Woodburners, Trottiscliffe, Maidstone, Kent ME19 5EB Page 77
Aga-Rayburn, PO Box 30 Ketley, Telford, Shropshire TF1 1BR Page 74
Allia (UK) Ltd., Whieldon Road, Stoke on Trent ST4 4HN Page 100, 102/103
Alno, Unit 10, Hampton Farm Ind. Est., Hanworth, Middx TW13 6BD Page 84, 91, 96, 98
Antenna, 1 Rosemont Road, London NW3 Page 86/87
Antiference Ltd., Bicester Road, Aylesbury, Bucks HP19 3BJ Page 139
Armitage Shanks Ltd., Armitage, Rugeley, Staffs WS15 4BT Page 109

B
B C Sanitan, 30/31 Lyme St., London NW1 0EE Page 105
Beaver and Tapley, Scotts Rd., Southall, Middx 4B2 5DJ Page 61
BEHR Furniture, 51 Christchurch Rd., East Sheen, London SW14 7AQ Page 63
B.H. Stores PLC, Marylebone House, 129 Marylebone Rd., London NW1 5QD Page 57, 185
British Gypsum, Westfield, 360 Singlewell Rd., Gravesend, Kent DA11 7RZ Page 145, 146/147
British Telecom Page 65
Burg Bathrooms at Pipedreams, 103 Regents Park Rd., London NW1 Page 114/115

C
Calor Gas Ltd., Appleton Park, Slough, Berks SL3 9JG Page 30, 68
Countryside Masonry Ltd., Okus, Swindon, Wilts SN1 4JJ Page 175, 180, 181, 183
Crosby Kitchens, Orgreave Dr., Handsworth, Sheffield, S13 9NS Page 59, 85

D
Dorma, PO Box 7, Lees St., Swinton, Manchester, M27 2DD Page 127
Dow Corning Hansil, Wintersells Rd., Byfleet, Surrey, KT14 7LH Page 53, 54

F
Forbo Nairn, PO Box 1, Kirckcaldy, KY1 2SB Page 152
Fordham Bathrooms & Kitchens Ltd., Dudley Rd., Wolverhampton WV2 4DS Page 122, 110/111

G
G Plan, E. Gomme Ltd., PO Box 27 High Wycombe, HP13 7AD Page 67
Gyproc Glass Fibre Ins. Ltd., Whitehouse Ind. Est., Runcorn WA7 3DP Page 15

H
Halifax Building Society, Halifax Page 13
C.P. Hart & Sons Ltd., Newnham Terr., Hercules Rd., London SE1 7DR Page 108
Hepworth Iron Co. Ltd., Hazlehead, Stocksbridge, Sheffield Page 42, 44
House of Mayfair, Cramlington New Town, Northumberland NE23 8AQ Page 160, 162

I
ICI Dulux Paints, Wexham Road, Slough SL2 5DS Page 60, 62, 64, 126, 133, 134, 135, 139, 142, 153, 155, 157, 158
Ideal Standard Ltd., PO Box 60, National Avenue, Kingston upon Hull HU5 4JE Page 112

Jacket Design
Ivor Claydon/Bob Hook
Sunset Design Company Limited

Jacket Photography
Graham Miller